PUBLIC POLICY

Formulation Implementation Analyses
PAKISTAN FOCUSED

By
SARFRAZ KHAWAJA

Ph.D University of Missouri, Columbia (USA)

www.mrbooks.com.pk
Email: mrbooks@isb.comsats.net.pk

Published by Mohammad Eusoph, Mr. Books,
Super Market, Islamabad, Pakistan
Ph: +92-51-227 8843 – 45 Fax: +92-51-227 8825

Title designed by Zulfiqar Ali Joya

Printed and Bound in Pakistan by:
Pictorial Printers (Pvt) Ltd.
Islamabad – Pakistan
Tel: +92-51-260 3108 / 09

Cataloguing in Publication Data
Main Entry under Author

Khawaja, Sarfraz

   Public Policy: Formulation Implementation Analyses. – Islamabad:
Mr. Books.

1. Political Planning-Pakistan   2. Policy Formation
3.   Policy Implementation   4. Implementation Analysis

320.65491   ISBN: 978-969-8121-08-2

Price:	Pakistan	Foreign
	Rs.1060	US$ 20

This book is dedicated to my mentor

Professor N.G. Barrier (late),
Dean,
School of Art & Sciences,

University of Missouri,
Columbia, USA.°

_____

PREFACE

Public Policy does not have teeth but it bites' Is that what happens? Pakistan is in a perpetual state of slide and is facing existential crises where the Max Weber's principles of political economy would seem to be helpless. During the last ten years since 2000, Country is groaning under huge pressure of socio-economic decline. By the end of June 2013, Pakistan is burdened with US$60.87 billion foreign debt and Rupees 8,800 billion of internal debt. Foreign investment has declined to US$ 853 million from US$3.7 billion in 2008. The foreign exchange reserves with the Central Bank amounts to US$ 6.5 billion which is barely enough for 60 days of imports. During the next 12 months, US$ 5 billion had to be given back to IMF as loan repayment. The GDP ratio is 3.7% whereas inflation is 9%. The country is also facing trade deficit of US$ 12.54 billion. The stuck up loans of local banks have amounted to the tune of one trillion rupees. Is this enough of biting?

This is only part of economic mismanagement notwithstanding the bad governess, thousands of lives lost in terrorist attacks, deteriorating general crime situation and above all the massive corruption in the public sector organizations, miss-management in government offices and institutions. The extreme shortage of gas, petrol and electricity particularly for industry and ordinary household has demonstrated the negligence and inefficiency of the government. The entire country suffers from electricity load shedding of 16 hours or more in 24 hours depending on geographical proximity of the resident. The province of Punjab is the worst hit and the province of Sindh is the least sufferer. This all happened in the presence and declaration of different public policies of several ministries, sectors and departments including monetary and fiscal policies announced from time to time with regular intervals.

What happens if there is no public policy? The solace is far away because the non policy situation is no better option than the declared bad Policy. The awful governance, poverty, unemployment, target killings in Karachi, unrest in Baluchistan and above all USA Drone attacks and so on are the results of no public policies. Pakistan has been a very serious victim of terrorist activities since 2000 but unfortunately no policy stipulation has been enacted as a Policy against Terrorism.

Who is responsible for the lack of policy formulation on critical areas such as anti terrorism, security (especially human security plus external security) power shortage, food security and several others?

Is it legislature (mostly politicians), executive (bureaucracy) Judiciary (apex Courts) or all powerful institution (armed forces)? All of them are equally responsible because each of privileged and powerful key stake holders preferred to stay in their comfort zones. Was it done intentionally or because of poor understanding about the policies of the country and its implication?

It resonates that Pakistan is not short of public policies. That may be the situation if the policy is seen as hybrid declaration of reactive statements by the Chief Executive or Head of the State. Public policy is a sacred trust, a commitment of the stake holders and an instrument of public support for the well being of its people and advancement of the country. If these two things do not combine then the policy existence is farce and misleading.

There has been rampant corruption in Pakistan. It is assumed that in most of the cases it is greed factor and in rare situation need factor can be seen. In reality corruption is system based in Pakistan. Hence it needs systemic remedy. But no consistent anti- corruption policy has been developed and even if there are some announcements in bits and pieces against corruption the implementation is haphazard.

In most of the developing countries like Pakistan public policy has been used as a vehicle of growth and hardly entailed change. This is also correct in most of the policies related to different ministries and departments. This was because of the legacy of colonial rule in which social institutions and state policy were used as an instrument of repression to perpetuate power. Every situation was perceived as a law and order problem which could disrupt the revenue collection by the state apparatus.

The excitement of independence and sovereignty was so over whelming that structure and design of social institutions and public policy were not modified. The changed status of the society, not only in geographical sense, but more so in the context of social, political and economic development, the needed institutions to meet the demands of a new country were neither created nor developed.

The needs and expectations of the new polity were not compatible with the existing state institutions. The resulting chaos and mismanagement is the manifestation of conflict between the development process which presupposes to work for societal needs and the state policy which is dominated to protect the interest of elite groups. The state institutions whether dealing with the governance of the masses or the dispensation of justice, the operations of finances or the functions of civic amenities worked primarily through force, coercion, nepotism or any other such means.

The long years of master subject relationship with little sharing of authority with people has resulted in a psyche which has become intolerant, short tempered and confrontationist. These tendencies run through in all the facets from politics to family life. The roles of social institutions were relegated to authoritarian culture fully supported by the state power.

As a result this institutional structure did not take cognizance of the demands of the independence which brought socio political awakening in the people. This situation of a strange anomaly was created which needs corrective actions through the democratization of social institutions.

Do the existing social institutions and public policy match the needs of changing realities of our society? The answer is an embarrassing No.

The public policy and social institutions working coherently provide structure to the society to make the life of its people organized, manageable and generally satisfied. Hence the rules of business of these institutions have to be framed and practiced in a judicious way to accommodate the needs, requirements and aspirations of the people who are being governed by these institutions. The conflict arose because of the use of discretionary authority without judicious interpretation. The results have been:

i) Failure of the institutions in the achievement of its objectives,

ii) Reaction by the polity rendered the institutions ineffective and redundant.

It is imminent that planners, managers, administrators and implementers need to be qualified and trained in public policy formulation, implementation and analysis. It is obvious that rules of business for managing the human resources have to be different than plastic commodities. This leads to the domain of human relations, communication, motivation and discipline. There are several options to resolve conflict situations which will lead to consensus building on institutional basis.

But this change needs more than rhetoric. It needs a change of attitude. Human attitudes and behaviors do not change easily, since they are firmly rooted in their psyche. If we intend to change the behavior of our management structures we will have to scientifically organize and affect a meaningful change in our human resource departments who are responsible for formulation, implementation and analysis of public policy and social institutions.

The early draft of this book was read by Dr. Ghais ul Haq, Masood Muzaffar and Asad Wahidi. Masood examined and analyzed the manuscript thoroughly despite his overseas travel commitments. It helped to improve the draft and challenged some assumptions. Asad also examined the draft as a keen analyst and provided useful interventions some of which have been included. I am appreciative of their time, effort and help.

I am grateful to Dr. Zahid Hussain for the final editing of this book. Having said all that, I would appreciate candid comments from readers on this modest though challenging effort.

My special thanks are due to Zulfiqar Ali Joya and Muhammad Usman Gujjar for the great pains they took in composing, formatting and presenting this book. However, I am solely responsible for any errors or omissions in this book.

Dr. Sarfraz Khawaja
sarfrazshk@yahoo.com
Cell: +92-51-333-435-7675

CONTENTS

Chapter = 3
POLICY FORMULATION 74

Chapter = 4
POLICY IMPLEMENTATION 94

Chapter = 5

POLICY ANALYSIS   120

1

PUBLIC POLICY

Can we define it?

The definition of any subject in Social Sciences, has remained a tricky issue in the past and would likely to remain so in the future. This lack of uniform definition has its own merits. The attempts by the scholars and professors to adhere to one specific definition in social sciences have not yet succeeded. Its key merit is the constant effort by all concerned to keep on devising clarity and meaningfulness to one definition. This effort and changing circumstances of different societies and nations has enriched the field of social sciences. Hence public policy is not an exception to this practice and recognition.

The genesis of Public Policy as an independent discipline has been of recent emergence. Traditionally Public Policy was a sub discipline of political science and was taught / researched in Universities/Colleges under political science. It is not more than few decades ago that public policy has emerged as a distinct discipline which is analyzed and explained as an academic discipline. Several

Universities have established new or separate Departments or Schools of Public Policy. One such example is the establishment of "Lee Kuan Yew School of Public Policy" in Singapore. Similarly in Pakistan "National School of Public Policy" at Lahore has been working for few years, primarily discharging the functions of in-service training to middle and senior level bureaucrats. It has yet to launch a degree program in Public Policy. Several universities and institutes of higher education all over the world has established independent departments of Public Policy in North America, Europe, Asia and other parts of the world. This has given impetus to the study of Public Policy and wider choices to students of public administration to benefit from new vistas and knowledge in policy formulation, implementation and analysis.

"Aristotle dispatched his assistants to collect the constitutions of over one hundred city states, which he then compared to derive general political principles. Writers in ancient Greece and Rome commonly distinguished system of governments in terms of both who ruled (one person, an elite few or the many) and the principles by which they actually exercised their power (whether in their own interests or for the good of the whole). It was the principles behind courses of action that separated monarchy from tyranny, aristocracy from oligarchy, democracy from despotic mob rule"[1].

In the ancient times political principles were compared to derive conclusions which policies would be appropriate for the benefit of the people at large. This could well be termed as comparative analysis of different systems and policies for the purpose of devising most useful course of action for a state. But in this endeavor the interests of the rulers were not sacrificed. It is because of this approach that the histories of countries and states are laden with kings and rulers; how they occupied the throne or power; why the wars of succession were fought; how brutally the prince and monarchs were killed as and when power becomes the main desire and focus of life. The life and history of people were not significant in the context policy formulation and implementation. This practice continued for a long time and change became possible during the 17th century and then in the 18th century with the advent of French Revolution.

The "Kautiliya Arthasatra" is perhaps the oldest treatise on the governance and administrative practices for a State. It was written between 321-296 BC in the Sanskrit language by 'Kautiliya' and subsequently translated into several languages. In its section 1 Chapter Four entitled "i) Establishing (the necessity of) Economics and Science of Politics" has been mentioned "the three Vedas and economics is the Rod (wielded by the king); its administration constitutes the science of politics, having for its purpose the acquisition of (things) not possessed, the preservation of (things) possessed, the augmentation of (things) preserved and the bestowal of (things) augmented on a worthy recipients. ii) Therefore, the (king), seeking the orderly maintenance of worldly life, should ever hold the

Rod lifted up (to strike). For, there is no such means for the subjugation of beings as the Rod, say the (ancient) teachers.

iii) No, says Kautilya. For, the (king), severe with the Rod, becomes a source of terror to beings. The (king), mild with the Rod, is despised. The (king), just with the Rod, is honoured. iv) For, the Rod, used after full consideration, endows the subjects with spiritual good, material well-being and pleasures of the senses. Used unjustly, whether in passion or anger, or in contempt, it enrages even forest. If not used at all, it gives rise to the law of the fishes. For, the stronger swallows the weak in the absence of the wielder of the Rod. Protected by him, he prevails. v) the people, of the four 'varnas' and in the four stages of life, protected by the king with the Rod, (and) deeply attached to occupations prescribed as their special duties, keep to their respective paths."[2]. This applies more in the context of implementation of government or state decisions but simultaneously implementation of public policy remains an important segment of the government responsibility. It can be deducted that the policies and regulations of the state were clearly laid down and so was the enforcement of their rules and policies from ancient time. This demonstrates that politics and economics travelled side by side to the present time and in more sophisticated term it is known as political economy, which sometimes is also referred as real politics.

The perennial demand of Islamic treatise is that the principles of morality remain the foundation of any policy which is inclusive of Public Policy. This concept has to be practiced in all walks of life, be it Politics, Economics,

Sociology or Scientific research. Any political, administrative and national expediency can never tolerate any fraud, injustice or falsehood. This has to be practiced "whether it be relations between the ruler and ruled within the state, or the relations of state with other states, precedence must always be given to truth, honesty and justice over material considerations. It imposes similar obligations on the state as on the individuals, viz: to fulfill all contracts and obligations, to have uniform standards for dealing; to remember duties along with the rights and not to forget the rights of others when expecting them to fulfill their obligations; to use power and authority for the establishment of justice and not for the perpetration of injustice".[3]

The key injunctions in the Islamic policy is the pursuit and deliverance of Justice which runs across with equal obligation rather compulsion for the individuals, group of people, family life, society, nation, state and encompassing all these in the form of a geographical proximity which can be called a country. Hence the fundamental policy principle is unambiguous but lacks implementation. Besides, the fundamentals of morality need to be enshrined in the norms and practice in a sovereign state. But these basis would be established in such a way that the country would practice the principles of a welfare state not only in words but also in deeds. That is the crux of policy principles which not only stops the nations to stumble but also provide road map for future course of action.

The general principles of power politics were unearthed in the Sixteenth Century by the intense efforts of Niccolo Machiavelli. He provided down-to-earth policy advice to princes. Machiavelli was a political theorist and lived in Italy during the Renaissance period in the beginning of the 16th century. He was also a contemporary of another greater Leonardo de vinci. Itlay was not a single at that time and Machiavelli was a civil servant for the Florentine Republic in the northwest. This city state was in a continuous and linger state of political unrest. In this backdrop, he wrote his treatise now known as The Prince in which he presented his theory as to how a prince could ensure long term political control and power in turbulent times. In precise terms 'The Prince' is a step by step book of devious instructions for all politicians. The book is not limited for use to politicians but it also extends to all those who went to seek and hold power within a family, work peace, professional group, social enterprise, political party or government. The dubious use of diplomacy, flattery, bribery, corruption, illegal gratification, misinformation with a disposition which entails charm and charisma were all the means to ensconce oneself in position of lasting power and control. In chapter 5 of the treatise "How such cities and principalities are to be governed who lived under their own laws before they were subdued: It has been mentioned" when states that are newly conquered have been accustomed to their liberty, and lived under their own laws to keep them three ways are to be observed: the first is utterly to ruin them; the second, to live personally among them; the third is (contenting yourself with a pension from them) to permit them to enjoy their old privileges and laws, erecting a kind of council of state, to consist of a few which may have a care of your interest and keep the people in amity and obedience. And that council being setup by you, and knowing that it subsists only by your favor and authority, will not omit anything that may propagate and enlarge them".[4]

If we put this in simple words in the context of public policy it means that through careful considerations of actions and reactions it should be possible to manipulate circumstances to ensure a continuation of rule. The concept and notion of honesty, morality, ethics, temperance, moderation, legitimacy etc. must all be knit into one paradigm that is the control and perpetuation of power and authority. If this approach is pursued and managed it would secure the power and dominance of 'The Prince' which is the ultimate end to be achieved. This idea of planning ahead and analyzing circumstances was not common place in the 15th and 16th century hence. Machiavelli's approach was considered revolutionary and practiced even today.

Analysis of different concepts reveals a diversity of definitions. Some are very broad in nature and others boil down to interpretations which are quite narrow and skewed. The policy statement is not the only objective of Public Policy. There are other covert or subconscious objectives. Anderson defines the parameters of policy as:

- Being goal oriented rather random, although goals could be loosely stated and unclear.

- Consisting of courses or patterns of action taken over time by government official rather than discrete, separate decisions.
- Involving what governments do, not what they intend to do, including policy outputs in pursuance of policy decisions and statements.
- Being accepted as legitimate, authoritative and legally based.[5]

Another set of public policy writers defines policy in a definitive way. Turner and Hulme elaborate policy in variety and ranges which include:

- Specific proposal: To reduce inflation by three percent in the next year.
- Decisions of government: Policy decisions announced by the president or parliament.
- A specific program: Land reform program.
- Output: What is actually delivered such as the number of subsidies given?
- Outcome: What is actually achieved such as better health care for women?
- A theory or model: If we do X then what will happen?: or if people have clean water there will be lower mortality rate.
- Process: A long term matter, which begins with issues and moves through objective setting, decision making, implementation and evaluation.[6]

Here the question can be raised as how the Pakistan parliament knows about the effectiveness of policy implementation? The logical response is, that the agency or agencies which have been made responsible to monitor, evaluate and measure the process, output and outcomes of policy implementation should report to the parliament. It is the Planning Commission in the case of Pakistan which monitors and evaluates projects, programs and policies. Hence the planning commission through the office of its Deputy Chairman (Status of Federal Minister) report to the parliament. Another watchdog is Public Accounts Committee (PAC) which consists of parliamentarian both of treasury and opposition benches to scrutinize the financial part (Expenditure) of policy implementation and makes administrative ministries / departments accountable for the wrongful expenditure.

There is another set of variables provided by Bridgeman and Davis that elaborates policy:

- Is international, designed to achieve a stated or understood purpose
- Involves decisions and their consequences
- Structured and orderly
- Political in nature
- Dynamic[7]

However a more coherent definition comes from Davis...... "Public Policy is the complex interplay of values interests and resources. Policy express values support or curtail interest and distribute resources. They shape and are shaped by the constituent elements of politics so that policies represent victories or compromises encapsulated as programs for action by government".[8]

It is a common practice that government stipulate policies, enact laws, allocate resources, establish or modify necessary infrastructure and above all demonstrate resolve to formulate and implement policies. In addition to government; Individuals, Professional groups, Civil Society organization, Community based organization and other interest groups attempt to shape Public Policy through education, information, communication, advocacy and mobilization but the key responsibility of implementation or service delivery remains with the government. But the overriding basis of legitimacy for Public Policy is the enactment of law and unless it is stipulated the policy lacks the desired competency for implementation.

Why Study Public Policy?

The question can thus be asked as to why the institutes of Public Policy gained so much currency recently and in elaborate fashion as the full-fledged graduate schools have been established of Public Policy. There are several reasons for this change. The most demanding cause of this change is the growing disenchantment of the people/masses at large of developed or developing countries. Generally speaking the inactions of governments to stipulate appropriate policies for particular country have caused more damage than enunciating weak/poor Public Policy. This can be understood and explained by the damaging power shortage in Pakistan. The generation of electricity in

January 2012 is 10,280 MW. This capacity would have been increased by more than 70% with the existing infrastructure, manpower and good governance. As such the available electricity generation would be 17,476 MW which exceeds existing demand of 14,980 MW for Pakistan. However the power generation policy failed because of several reasons some of which include; Poor policy formulation, short sighted vision, bad management and dismal implementation. The demand of electricity in January 2012 was 14980 MW per day. Pakistan generates electricity by following means:-

Hydel	2600MW
Thermal	1800MW
Independent power projects (IPP)	5880MW
Total	**10280MW**

The daily electricity shortfall was 4700 MW. However variation for each day in power generation and demand keep on fluctuating based on the reason, weather condition, power consumption, but not withstanding line losses, bad governance, wastage, and use of government resources for personal gains.

The installed capacity of Hydel stations in operation is 6,516 MW but electricity generation is only 2600 MW which is about 40% of the capacity. If the gap between capacity and generation is minimized it would provide more energy to the industry for better economic growth.

The Water and Power Development Authority (WAPDA) prepared a Hydropower generation plan from 2007-2025. It has been estimated that by 2025 the Peak demand of electricity in Pakistan would be 58,015 MW and the installed capacity of Hydropower generation would be 35,412 MW. The gap of 23,403 MW would be met from other sources of power generation including thermal, wind, nuclear etc. The estimated cost of Hydropower generation would be US$ 47.8 Billion by 2025. But there is a caveat, that is, subject to the arrangement of required funds and fulfillment of all formalities. However there is another element which is the management and technical capacity of the prevailing administrative system. The availability of funds does not ensure that the output and outcome would match the objectives and goals.

The inaction on the part of the Government of Pakistan was not to build Hydel power projects despite the availability of abundant water which could have been in lakes. Hence water played havoc in the form of floods and then water flowed to the sea. Instead a wrong or a bad policy of thermal power plants were started. As a result thermal power can only be run by oil which has to be imported by Pakistan. The country imports about 85% of oil for its needs whereas hydro electricity would have been quite feasible and affordable option. This inaction as well as bad policy has damaged the Pakistan economy by selecting the wrong option of thermal electricity. Hence it can be devised that any action or inaction on the part of the government which effects, directly or indirectly, negatively or positively, major part of the population can be termed as Public Policy. But this does not exclude the minority groups or vested interests suffering or benefiting by the Public Policy. However the central idea in policy science is that it entails several options or choices to determine policy alternatives. But in organized working system / society inaction is not considered an option in the modern context.

"As Social Science does more analysis of hypotheses, predictions, causation and optimizing, there develops a body of potential premises that can be used in deducting conclusions, just as chemistry was able to deduce the existence of new elements before they were empirically discovered"[9].

By the same token policy sciences include different methods/models by which the Policy processes is investigated. Public Policy is not based on abstract notions or whims rather it is a well thought out processes planned in such a way for certain outcomes. Although the implementation of Public Policy may not always match the expected outcomes but it must determine the policy direction in a broader context. If this direction is missing or extremely abstract then there is a likely hood that the policy has failed to lay the fundamentals of policy directions and worst still more would be its disastrous implementation. Thus it is imminent that Public Policy must be an outcome of Scientific Planning. Hence inaction on the part of the government / state cannot be called a Public Policy.

"Public Policy is whatever governments do or not do. Governments do many things. They regulate conflict within society; they organize society to carry or conflict with other societies, they distribute a great variety of symbolic rewards and material services to members of the society and they extract money from society, most often in the form of taxes. Thus public policies may regulate behavior, organize bureaucracies, distribute benefits, or extract taxes – or all these things at once."[10]

Another useful part of defining the Public Policy also reveals that government respond to some of the demands placed upon it, but some are ignored and neglected being considered as less important and few others may attract quick response.

"The notion of non-decision is one to explain why some issues don't get heard. Non-decision making is a means of preventing issues from entering the political process altogether. There is a considerable debate over the issue of non-decision making. Some viewpoints are that i) It is impossible to study what does not occur ii) Non-decision making is actually decision making – there are powers that are actively suppressing issues from being discussed or heard"[11].

Government Expansion

The deprivation of masses in developing countries is enormous. Even the basic needs of food, shelter and health facilities are few and inefficient hence people demand from the government to provide the basic necessities. The availability of education facilities, poor sanitation and potable water is hardly available to 50% of the population in Pakistan. The demand for these necessities of life further increased due to unmanageable population growth rate of 2.8% per annum. The financial resource constraints and massive corruption depletes the resources and hampers development efforts. As a result large segment of population live below the poverty line which is demonstrated by the following table.

Table – 1: Population living below US$ 1.25 per day (poverty line)

Country	Total Population in millions	Percentage of Population living below poverty line
India	1241	41.6
Pakistan	176	22.6
Bangladesh	150	49.6
Sri Lanka	21	7.0
Malaysia	28	0.0
Indonesia	242	18.7
Nepal	30	Not available

Source: UNDP, Human Development Index: 2009: New York

The demand of more basic needs is genuinely required which provide the government an opportunity to expand the number of Ministries, Department, Offices and hire more personnel at all levels of the rung. Sometimes this becomes counterproductive because the expansion of administrative machinery does not necessarily provide efficient service delivery through Public Policy. The expenditure of the government increases in less productive activities such as construction of very ambitious transportation projects, purchase and even import of expansive furniture which hardly provide solace to the deprived people.

A considerable segment of population even in developed countries demand and expect from government to solve their problems. They desire over the years that public policy should be designed to alleviate personal discomforts or un-societal unease. During the last 60 years the governments in Pakistan have expanded in size which does not necessarily mean that this growth was in consonance with gross domestic product (GDP). Following figure explain the situation in the context of Pakistan.

Table – 2: Percentage GDP growth and increase in Public Sector Program

Year	Percentage growth of GDP *	Percentage growth of Public sector Personnel *[1]
1960	6.8%	8% *[2]
1970	4.8%	7%
1980	6.5%	8%
1990	4.6%	6%
2000	4.8%	7%
2010	3.1%	10%
2012	3.0%	10%

*: Government of Pakistan: Finance Division: Pakistan Economic Survey 2011-2012 (Economic & Social Indicators): Islamabad 2012: p2

*[1]: Any definitive information on the growth of public sector personnel is not available despite the efforts to find out from different Ministries and the personnel (officers and officials) working there. Hence it has been derived from different segments of data loosely available in different Ministries and departments. This information in the column is a combination of guess and estimate hence guesstimation. Further reliable figures would be welcome.

*[2]: These are physical numbers in percentages and not financial outlays. If it is juxtaposed with the financial allocations / expenditure then the increase would be much higher.

The causality of relationship between growth of personnel and GDP reflects that the expansion of government is much rapid. Similarly the budget of different ministries increased rapidly but the Human Development Indicators has improved slowly.

Table – 3: Budget Expenditure (Ministry-wise) and Percentage Increase

	2009 (Rs. Million)	2010 (Rs. Million)	Percentage increase
Defense *	342,486	405,698	18.46
Education	6,300	7,511	19.22
Health	16,538	22,875	32.27
Women Development	155	226	45.81

Source: Government of Pakistan, Controller General of Accounts:- Financial Statements of the Federal Government: Financial Year 2009-10: Islamabad: 2010: p29-30

*: There is lot of hidden expenditure but perhaps that cannot be alluded to.

It is evident from the above table that the increase in the expenditure for the ministry of Women Development was more than 45% in one year as against the increase in the defence budget which was about 18% which was three times less. But the difference of amount in the base year (e.g.2009) was enormous between defence and Women Development. In figures, the Defence expenditure was 2210 times more if compared with women development. Although during the next year 2010, the gap decreased but it was still quite high and that was 1795 times more. This is a simplistic comparison. The resources spent on education, health, environment even defence are also incurred on women. It is not fair to bracket the gender issues with one ministry. The percentage increase in the education expenditure is 'quite low among the above cited four sectors which are 19%. Here again the base amount is quite small as compared to defence. The need of education and health sectors are enormous to uplift the Human Development Indicators. This is not being done and it nosedived in the last five years hence the results are reflected as below, notwithstanding other reasons and the top of the list is corruption and bad governance.

Table – 4: Human Development Indicators and Percentage Achievement

Indicators	2009	2010	Percentage achievement
Under five mortality rate (per 1000 live birth)	78	73	6.41
Infant mortality rate (per 1000 live birth)	66	62	6.06
Maternal mortality ratio (per 100,000 live birth)	240	220	8.33
Literacy rate *	57%	58%	1.75
Net primary enrollment	57%	56%	-1.75

Source: Government of Pakistan, Economic Survey of Pakistan: 2011-2012: Islamabad: p138, 139, 151

*: The definition of literacy in vogue at international level is 'Reading, Writing and Comprehension'. Another complexity is further added to this definition which includes 'life skills'.

The Human Development Report of United Nations Development Program (UNDP) for the year 2013 has been released in the last week of March, 2013. The Human Development Index (DHI) has dropped to 146th position in 2013 from 127th of last year. Pakistan's expenditure on social sectors in lower than some of the poor African countries like Congo which spends 1.2% of GDP on Health

(0.8 % for Pakistan) and 6.2% on Education (1.8% for Pakistan) Brazil, one of the highest HD performing countries, spends 4.25% on health and 5.7% on education. The key reason, identified by the report, for Pakistan is the lack of continuity in public policies for long term Development.

Importance of Public Policy

Traditionally the public policy had been a part rather a smaller segment of Political Science. Political Science is a study of Politics with focus on political process, political parties, elections and voting, lobbying, legislation and in certain ways government institutions. The last part falls in the domain of Public Policy which provides description and explanation of the causes and consequences of government activity. The policy studies in the latter half of the 20th century were mostly dominated by socio-economic theories. The post World War-II era was loaded with this approach primarily because of the emerging socio-economic realities and the devastations caused by the war which have effected most of the nations in the world.

The Marshall Plan (an economic development model), North Atlantic Treaty Organization (NATO) an outfit for defense control policy mechanism primarily for the protection of Western Europe but subsequently extended to wherever USA desired, the culmination of WARSAW pact, a command response by USSR to protect Eastern Europe and several other such policies were primarily for economic growth. The financial benefits of war Industry worked well both for USA and USSR. These policies generated opportunities for economic growth and industrialization but also created environmental dislocations and hazards, health issues and other defense related complications of Nuclear Proliferation with the immense growth of economies. As a result the Governments of different countries were caught in the imperatives of capitalist accumulation on the one hand and workers and their representatives / unions on the other.

"This involves a description of the content of public policy; an analysis of the impact of social, economic and political forces on the content of Public Policy, an inquiry into the effect of various institutional arrangements and political processes on Public Policy and an evaluation of the consequences of public policy on society both expected and unexpected." [12]

The importance of studying public policies has a broader agenda but there are several compelling reasons that public policies should be properly understood through scientific analysis and modern day evaluation techniques and methods. The importance of Public Policy in a broader sense, which covers different economic and social policies but also include foreign and defense policies reflects the overall development status of a country. Well formulated and efficiently implemented Public Policies ensure diligence, transparency, accountability rule of law, fair play and level playing field for people at large. In case of Pakistan especially since 2000 the Public Policies have been badly prepared and poorly implemented notwithstanding the massive financial and political corruption, bad governance and illegal gratification. In this chaos the economy of the country was affected in the worst manner. The major public sector institutions are on the verge of collapse. These include Pakistan Railways, Pakistan International Airlines, Oil and Gas Regularity authority, Power generation systems, Pakistan Steel Mills and many others. As a result the macroeconomic indicators are in worst shape. The budget deficit during the last five years is an example of this morass.

Table – 5: Budget Deficit of Pakistan

Fiscal Year	Budget Deficit
2011-12	8.5%
2010-11	6.6%
2009-10	6.3%
2008-09	5.2%
2007-08	7.4%

Source: Pakistan Summary of Consolidated Federal and Provincial Budgetary Operation[13]

Figure - 1

Why Study Public Policy?

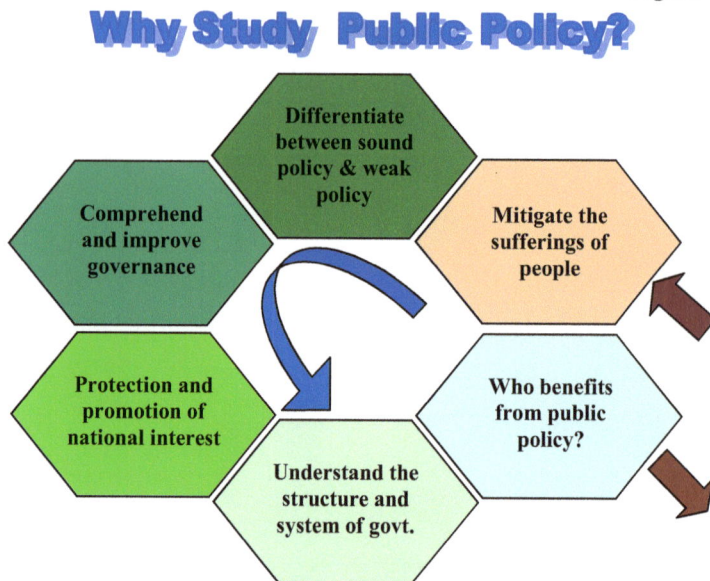

- Differentiate between sound policy & weak policy
- Comprehend and improve governance
- Mitigate the sufferings of people
- Protection and promotion of national interest
- Understand the structure and system of govt.
- Who benefits from public policy?

i) *Mitigate the sufferings of people*

The governments in different countries all over the world design public policies to mitigate the sufferings of its people and to protect the National interest of the country. The defense policy in particular addresses the issue of foreign threats but to a minor extent internal security issues. The economic policy (both Fiscal and Monetary) are directed mostly for the well being of its people and use the resources for the welfare of deprived classes and provide better access and opportunities to the poor specially living below the poverty line.

ii) *Difference between sound policy and weak policy*

The policy comparisons and analysis differentiate between sound policies and hurriedly prepared or weak policies. If this difference is not understood then you cannot differentiate between success and failure. If you cannot do this then you cannot punish the wrong and reward the success. It often happens that a sound policy is badly implemented which becomes a policy failure that results into lot of resource wastage, heavy burden on the exchequer, add frustration for the government and increase the sufferings of the people. It happens, though not very often, that a good policy is also implemented well and successfully. This brings confidence and efficiency in the working of the government machinery. But more important is that it mitigates the sufferings of the people and indicates improvement in the quality of life. This also establishes confidence in State Institutions.

The study and understanding of public policy is necessitated because of the importance it entails particularly it impacts a significant part of population of a country or it hinges upon the security and national interest of the state. Public Policy is not meant to identify certain pitfalls and failings of existing policy but it moves from diagnosis to prognosis, from theory to practical manifestation and from dreams to reality.

iii) Comprehend and improve governance
The implementation of Public Policies mostly revolves around the question of governance because of success or failure mostly hinges upon the quality of governance of the system or the ministry through which Public Policy is implemented. The question of governance is complex. It is often misunderstood as government and anything related to

governance is the responsibility of the government. Whereas governance is a management tool which is used in a creditable way by all the stakeholders which include Civil Society, different groups formed on the basis of profession, NGOs, CBOs and the people at large. But the key elements of governance remain Transparency, Accountability, Predictability and Participation. All these four indicators apply to all the actors and stakeholders of policy implementers.

iv) *Protection and promotion of national interest*

The protection and promotion of national interest, whether internal or external policy is referred, remains supreme however in actual practice it becomes quite intricate and complex because the country's policies do not work in isolation. A policy of one sector or ministry would have strong and varied implications on other policies. However, the key purpose of public policy is to find out viable options or undertake detailed problem solving techniques for national issues. Even if the problem is not resolved through Public Policy or the policy is pre-summed to be a failure even then it provides several lessons to be learnt. The policy makers, implementers and academicians involved in pure research or applied science can learn and broaden their understanding of particular policy problem. It also provides insight to test general theories, hypotheses and models of Public Policy and may produce certain choice of social or collective nature.

v)   Understand the structure and system of government

The study and analysis of public policy not necessarily answer all or some of the questions that have been raised by the policy makers, policy implementers or persons effected (beneficiaries or negatively affected) by the policy. But it can address (as to "how, why and to what effect) different political parties, while in government, pursue particular courses of action or inaction. The question of how, depends mostly on the structure and system of government. For instance a country under a military dictator (as has been the case in Pakistan for almost thirty years intermittently), the question of how remains mysteriously hidden or unknown. But to look at it in a more straight forward way it was one man the military dictator, controlled exclusively as how a policy would be formed, implemented and measured.

In today's world the example of North Korea, where one person makes decision, answer this question of how? In the centralized structure of government, which includes China, Russia and several other Eastern European countries there control mechanism is quite strong but broad based as how the interest groups and bureaucracies work. The states with federal system of government (USA, India) and countries with unitary structure (Britain, France) though varies in political formation but focus their output for the welfare of their people and promote and protect the national interest. The question of 'why' is also difficult to answer, it has been debated, asked and is being still probed as to why Pakistan joined USA's war on terror to attack

Afghanistan on the poor pretext of terrorism. The words "Poor pretext" has been particularly used because in the 9/11 attack on USA twin towers, there was not even a single person involved from Pakistan, Afghanistan and Iraq. Hence to answer the 'why' as it seems that in 2001 a military dictator was in power in Pakistan and it was necessary for his survival and to perpetuate his rule to join USA in the war and accrue financial benefits for himself and military which was his power base.

The final element of "to what effect" is generally understood or interpreted as the payoff for the country and in certain cases, the vested interests of the ruling elite which would constitute the political party in power, bureaucracy, interest groups and in some cases religious parties or groups. But the fundamental focus remains on that people are the best judge to determine the usefulness of a particular policy. Also people assess and evaluate the performance of the party in power as what the government is doing or not doing to them and for them.

vi) *Who benefits from Public Policy?*

If everybody is not benefited from the public policy, then at least nobody should suffer from the same policy. However the amount of benefit accrued from public policy varies from policy to policy and different segments of society. The very notion and spirit of public policy is to bring benefits to the maximum number of people, be it direct or indirect. The defence policy in Pakistan is often the target as being the protector of one of the largest armies in the world but at the same time it provides the maximum number of employment to the population most of which belong to the lower middle class specially in the ranks and files of the army. The armed forces provide very extensive health coverage to its serving and retired officers and officials. Similarly the primary education system is so large that the state has become the biggest employer of personnel working in primary education. The downside is that an inefficient primary education system has been enlarged at much bigger scale at the cost of quality education. It happens also that group of influential people or certain vested interests forced the government / political party in power to device or enact such a policy which benefits the rich. This often happens in the case of taxation policy, import / export duties and foreign exchange regulations. It usually is a short term measure to benefit small group of very influential people and soon that policy would be revoked once the benefits accrued to the target group.

References

[1] Heidenleimer, A.J. Heclo, H, Adams, C.T: Comparative public policy. The politics of social choice in America, Europe and Japan: New York: St Martin's press, Inc. 1990: Page 7.

[2] KAUTILIYA: Kautiliya Arthasatra: translated in English by R.P. Kangle; then translated in Urdu from English by Shan-ul-Haq Haqee: Karachi: Taxes Printers: 1991: p7.

[3] Siddiqi, M: Governance in Islam: New Dehli: Maxford Books: 2006: p67.

[4] Machiavelli, Niccolo: The Prince: London: Harper Collins: 2011: p21.

[5] Anderson J.E: Public Policy Making: An introduction: Boston: Honghton Mifflin: 1990: pp-6 – 8.

[6] Turner, M and D. Hulme: Governance, administration and development: Making the state work: London Macmillam: 1997: p59.

[7] Bridgeman, P. and G. Davis: Australian Policy handbook 2nd ed. Sydney: Allen and Unwin: 1998: p3.

[8] Allama Iqbal Open University: Islamabad: Commonwealth of Learning Executive MBA/MPA: Sc I Public Policy: Code 5572: 2004: p42.

[9] S.S. Nagel: The Policy Studies Handbook, Toronto: D.C. Heath & co. 1980: p 204.

[10] Dye, Thomas R.: Understanding Public Policy, Prentice Hall, New Jersey: Upper saddle River: 2002: p1.

[11] Han, C. and M. Hill: The Policy process in the modern capitalist state. Brighton: Wheatsheof: 1984: p65.

[12] Dye, Thomas R.: Understanding Public Policy: p4.

[13] Mahajir, Tanqueer: The NEWS International: Money Matters: Government's to do list: Lahore: p1.

2

PUBLIC POLICY MODELS
Do we need it?

In the standard text books on Public Policy it has been considered imminent to explain the Public Policy Models. These models are conceptual in nature but explained with such a purpose which helps to understand the importance of Public Policy but more important is that how different policies in varied situations and different countries can be analyzed. Before presenting the public policy Models it is quite important to know in more precise terms as to why these conceptual Models are necessary for policy analysis. There are four key reasons.

First: Politics and Public Policy has a congenital relationship because the Public Policy has been developed from the discipline of political science. Hence the politics and political science are the parents of Public Policy, Political Economy, Bureaucracy and many other aspects have emanated from* political science. Public Policy is not something which is only limited to conceptual model but it is a step forward to understand real politics. The Analysis and understanding of public policy would enable us to simplify and clarify our thinking of the concepts which would help in analyzing policy. By analyzing the models of Public Policy it enables the people at large who are affected by Public Policy (Positively or negatively) where and how different policies faulted and similarly how the vested interest, Elite groups and Bureaucracy manipulates the policy formulation, implementation, monitoring and evaluation. It often happen that sound policies (economically and socially) are badly implemented (administratively and politically) which leads to policy failure. One such example is the Madrassa Education Policy in Pakistan. This viable option to provide access to education to the poor people has been badly managed and politically exploited. This has led to policy failure. The detailed analysis of this policy should be presented in the later chapter to demonstrate that Madrassa Education Reform initiated by the Government of Pakistan created so much mistrust; even the welfare part of the policy looks harmful and unreasonable.

Second: There is no public policy which is problem free but every policy provides several lessons to be learnt once its implementation is started. The identification of problems is the first step in the policy formation mechanism. The common method used for problem identification is based on the input approach which means that what resources have been provided but not necessarily made available for policy implementation. The allocation of resources is not a good way to analyze and identify the problems because it only covers the supply side without analyzing or comparing with the demand side. The imbalance between the two is fraught with the handicap of wrong approach for problem identification. Hence there is a note of caution that the government or the public sector funded policies are often measured on the basis of resource allocation which is most of the cases are not available even up to 60% of the announced budget. On the other side it often happens that there has been too much focus on output which again is not a very rational approach. The policy output is measured against the laid down objectives of a given policy. The objectives are sometime hurriedly prepared with unrealistic targets. Also the objectives have been lofty almost unachievable and non-measurable. The lack of balance or synergy between the supply and demand sides makes the policy analysis even further complex to identify problems. It is one angle to look at the policy problem but the process which is the key element, between inputs and output is often ignored or given little importance. It is the policy processes which provide the key to understand the reasons of policy failure, poor implementation, success and partial success. This would identify the fault lines and provide timely opportunity to take corrective measures. However there is a note of caution that problem identification is not meant to prove the failure of policy but also provide clear reasons for policy improvement, modification and changes in the formulation and implementation of policy. In Pakistan the health policy of 1997 set targets for Infant Mortality rate to be brought down to 40 in 2003 and 20 in 2010. But the situation on the ground was 74 in 2011. In the same policy maternal mortality rate was to be brought down to 200 in 2003 and 90 in 2010. But the actual achievement in 2011 has been 300 from 350 in 1998. Similarly in the 2001 Health Policy, the target for immunization coverage was to be increased to 80% in 2005 and full coverage by 2010. But this could only reach at 60% in 2011. Now this does not identify the problem. It only tells shortfalls in achieving policy targets. It is the process which would identify and establish the problems. Hence the identification of policy problems is important to improve the processes with focus on different aspects, which includes financial, technical, manpower, and above all management.

Third: There is a very popular question asked as to why a particular public policy has been so badly formulated and equally poorly implemented? This leads us to suggest explanations for public policy and its consequences. Historically Pakistan has been generating electricity through Hydel system which was about 70% of its total production. This was primarily done because of the availability of abundance of water in the rivers and the cost of power generation was low. The remaining 30% of the power was generated through thermal mostly depended on imported and expensive oil. During the last fifteen years this balance has been offset and at present (2012) the power generation has been shifted to thermal by 70% and Hydel by 30%. This has been clearly a wrong or bad policy. The reason for this shift was political and provided the government and the political party in power to get kick backs from foreign firms who have been given contract to produce electricity through thermal system. Hence the electricity became expensive and the shortfall in the supply of electricity reached to about 4700 MW every day. There has been a constant problem of load shedding of 10 to 18 hours depending upon the area one resides. The rural areas are the worst hit which suffers 20 hours of load shedding in 24 hours. The consequence of a bad policy is so obvious that people are fed up and anger is visible on the streets through processions and burning of government offices responsible for the provision and distribution of electricity. The common target (if not the culprit) is Water and Power Development Authority (WAPDA).

A comparison is provided that over a period of time the Thermal generation of electricity got priority over the Hydel generation.

Comparison of Hydel vs Thermal Generation

Year	Hydel	Thermal	Total
1983	2547 (64%)	1407 (36%)	3954
1990	2897 (45%)	3512 (55%)	6409
2000	4825 (33%)	9619 (67%)	14444
2012	6516 (32%)	12376 (68%)	20443

The above table shows that in 1983 Hydel-Thermal mix ratio was 64%:36%. With the passage of time more thermal plants were installed as compared to Hydel generation. Hence Hydel-Thermal mix ratio has been reversed to 32:68 in the year 2012. It is indeed the result of poor policy planning as no major hydropower project had been initiated after commissioning of Mangla and Tarbela dams on major rivers. The electricity through thermal generation processes was procured as short to medium term measures during last 30 years. The main reason was that it took 2 to 3 years to install thermal plant, could be built at any convenient place wherefrom transmission line can be constructed very easily up to National Grid.

Major Hydropower Projects are long term Projects and take 8 to 12 years including investigation and construction time. These are built in hilly terrain which has comparatively difficult access and requires longer transmission lines to connect with National Grid.

Installation cost of thermal plant is less than Hydel plant. However generation cost of thermal plant is 6 to 10 time more than Hydel plant. This has been the reflection of poor policy planning.

Fourth: Several countries in varied circumstances announce policies. Some of these declarations are disguised in such a way to deceive or misguide the people. It usually is bluff either to gain time, divert attention from other serious issue, use it as a feeler to see the reaction of different segments of society and outside the country or to convert the announcements as a political rhetoric which reflects the desire of masses which they want to accomplish. One such policy (rhetoric) has been used in Pakistan is (Roti, Kapra, Mukan) Bread, Cloths and Housing since 1970. The bluff element of public policy is usually observed in foreign policy statements. This is common for hostile neighboring countries to use this tactic. This has also happened quite often between and among the big powers. The Cuba Missiles crisis is a classical example of bluff in the early 1960s at a place which was as big as a football ground. The Missile installation was photographed by USA which created a storm in Washington (Whitehouse, State Deptt, Pentagon etc). The USA told USSR about this dangerous and highly inflammatory move but USSR denied any such installation. The USA weighed its option of using diplomatic channels and use of all kinds of force including naval blockade, atomic attack or the beginning of disastrous third world war. The USA made all channels available and ready to combat USSR on the issue of missiles installation in Cuba and send a warning of forty eight hours to USSR to remove the missiles. The Russian bluff had to surrender against the carefully thought out policy of USA. The USSR accepted the installation of missiles in Cuba and agreed to remove those within a stipulated period.

Another classical case is the gas pipeline project between Pakistan and Iran. This has been formally signed between the two presidents on March 9, 2013 whereas the term of the parliament and ruling parties at the center completes on March 16, 2013. It has been projected a great step of economic cooperation, even at the annoyance of USA, between the two neighbours. But what is the objective situation which exists at present, is given in the box[1]. It is a ploy for election rhetoric. Is it a myth or reality?

PIPE DREAM

By
Dr. Farrukh Saleem

The good news is that the cost of the Pak-Iran gas pipeline has come down from $1.5 billion to $1.3 billion. The bad news is that neither Iran nor Pakistan has $1.3 billion. The good news is that President Zardari will be inaugurating the pipeline on Monday. The bad news is that a 'pipedream' is being inaugurated, not a pipeline.

There are two major prerequisites to building the pipeline: money and technology. There are two sources that have the money: Chinese banks and western financial institutions. There are two sources that have the required technology: Gazprom, the Moscow-based gas giant and western pipeline entities. On March 14, 2012, the Beijing-based Industrial and Commercial Bank of China Ltd (ICBC) backed out of a deal to finance the Pak-Iran gas pipeline. On May 14, 2012, Gazprom, the largest extractor of natural gas in the world, pulled out of the Pak-Iran pipeline project.

No money, no technology. All politics. Lately, the Americans seem to be ditching our president and our president is out with a double-edged sword: annoy the Americans and when the project actually fails the next rulers in Islamabad can be conveniently held responsible for the failure.

The Iranians are completely isolated and are therefore playing along pretending that they are still interacting with other countries of the world. On February 6, 2012, Iran defaulted on payments of wheat imports from Ukraine. On February 7, 2012, Iran defaulted on payments worth $144 million for rice shipments from India. Conclusion: Iran has no hard currency left in its reserves.

The good news is that Iran is desperate to deal with Pakistan. The bad news is that South Pars gas field's reserves are yet to be ratified by a third party. The good news is that Sui Northern and Sui Southern are charging us around $3.50 per unit of gas. The bad news is that Iranian gas price is pegged to the price of crude and at the current level Pakistani consumers would have to cough out around $13 per unit of Iranian gas. More recently, Pakistan has asked Iran to revise the price of gas downwards from 78 percent of crude to 70 percent of crude (Iran has refused to renegotiate the price downwards.)

On December 22, 2011, the National Bank of Pakistan (NBP), responsible for raising the rupee component of the project, informed the Economic Coordination Committee's (ECC) Steering Committee on Iran-Pakistan (IP) Pipeline that it had "branches in different countries of the world and therefore it feared that these branches could be closed due to US sanctions." Subsequently, the NBP pulled out of the project.

In December 2011, the Oil and Gas Development Company Limited (OGDCL) "already cash constrained due to the circular debt, said that its US investors had threatened to retreat if the company financed the IP gas pipeline project." Subsequently, OGDCL pulled out of the project.

The other good news is that our second-largest source of grant assistance is Saudi Arabia (America is the largest). The other bad news is that al-Mamlakah al-' Arabiyyah as-Su'udiyyah does not want Pakistan to trade with Iran.

Our pipedream fantasy; End tragedy solve the riddle; And dissipate ideals of indecision pipe; Pipedreams like these will; Cease and die unleashed.

Models of Public Policy

What is a model in the context of Public Policy? Is it problem free or flawless? The model is only a limited tool to assist and understand policy processes, its formulation, implementation, evaluation and reformulation. But it would at best remain a framework of theoretical model which has flaws when applied to real situations. Despite limitations, it still remains a useful tool for identifying parts of the policy making process. It also helps to understand the exploration of how policy is made and carried out. It is reiteration that models are important for policy analysis and policy options to provide solutions to problems with accuracy and subjected to empirical and analytical provision. Model is not a prescription for policy choices rather it provides description to select the best option in a given situation or particular circumstances.

There are eight identified Models of Public Policy used to understand the purpose and functions of Public Policy and often referred for policy analysis. There is no one model which has been used exclusively to formulate and implement public policy for one sector. The key reason is that all models are conceptual in nature but their manifestation lies in operationalizing them in different context and varied sectors. The understanding of conceptual models is very helpful to understand the nature, scope and purpose of public policy. This would be demonstrated in this book when some policies would be analyzed of different sectors but all specific to Pakistan.

- *Institutionalism:* Policy as institutional output
- *Process:* Policy as Political Activity
- *Rationalism:* Policy as Maximum Social Gain
- *Incrementalism:* Policy as variations on the past
- *Group Theory:* Policy as group Equilibrium
- *Elite Theory:* Policy as Elite Preference
- *Public Choice Theory:* Policy as collective decision making by self interested individuals
- *Game Theory:* Policy as rational choice competitive situations

Models of Public Policy

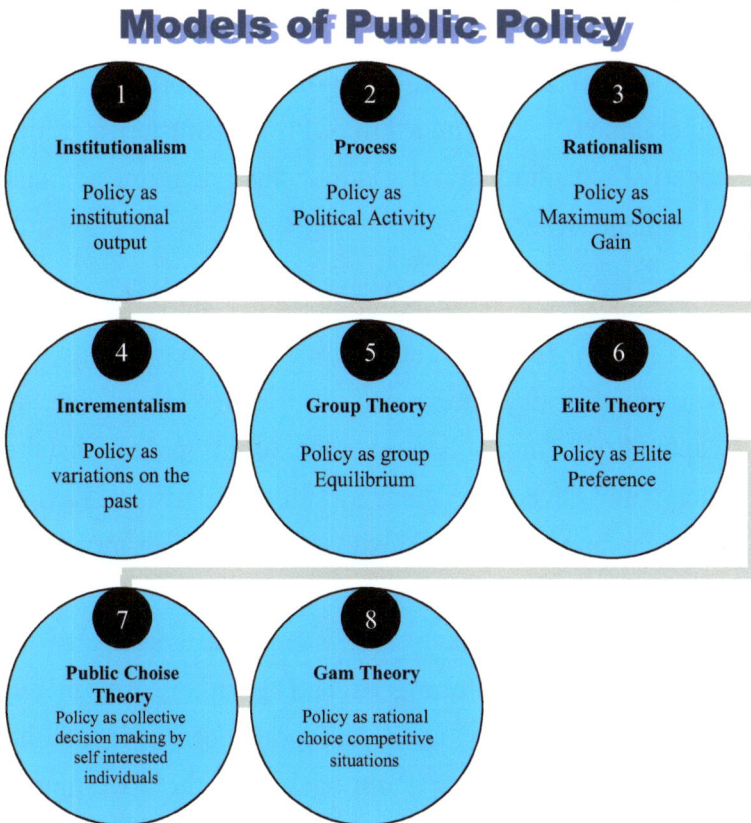

1 Institutionalism	2 Process	3 Rationalism
Policy as institutional output	Policy as Political Activity	Policy as Maximum Social Gain
4 Incrementalism	5 Group Theory	6 Elite Theory
Policy as variations on the past	Policy as group Equilibrium	Policy as Elite Preference
7 Public Choise Theory	8 Gam Theory	
Policy as collective decision making by self interested individuals	Policy as rational choice competitive situations	

1. *Institutionalization: Policy as Institutional Output*

Any policy either publicly announced by the government or otherwise conveyed cannot be called a public policy unless it is owned by the government. This ownership is not only a political rhetoric but it means that the government lends legitimacy to the policy through legislation. This is absolutely necessary so that the government policy becomes an obligation both for the government and people of a given country or state. It lends legitimacy for ownership, allocation of resources, supply of technical and qualified manpower, monitor and evaluate it and takes full responsibility of its success or failure. Legislation does not mean that each policy has to be backed by the Act of parliament. If a policy is approved by the cabinet under the chairmanship of Prime Minister (or Chief Executive Authority) it earns the legitimacy and government ownership.

Public policy involved universality in a sense that every citizen in that country or state recognizes the government policy irrespective of disagreement or its acceptability. This policy extends to all people in the society and everyone has to follow it even having disagreement and dislike. However this does not mean that the policy cannot be opposed. It can be challenged at the appropriate forum in a given system. The appeal can be launched in judicial forum, executive authority or in the legislature depending upon the point of view of the challenger. If any policy is not backed by the government then its appeal is limited to a small segment of society. It has weak appeal for implementation and also it losses credibility and acceptance. This argument can be further extended and explained that only government policy i.e. Public Policy, can be implemented through force of law, use of executive authority and even coercion. The policy violators can be imprisoned only by the government because the government is custodian of lawful authority. But legal procedure has to be followed. But governments do not hesitate to use authority or even high handedness to suppress the legitimate rights of people against corruption, price hike, poverty, dictatorial policies and alike.

The empirical question thus is that from where the federal or provincial (state) Governments derive independent legal authority. This emanates from the constitution of the state which is the law of the land. The constitution draws its authority from the citizens of the state which lends legitimacy and approval to the constitution. Once the constitution is approved by the representative of the citizens then it becomes the law of the land and provide a broader framework, role, responsibilities and authority of different institutions be it executive, legislature or judiciary. But the interpretation of the constitution is the exclusive authority of the higher judiciary in the country. This a normal practice but it is sometime violated by authoritarian rulers or military dictators. Hence it can be safely and strongly argued that the role of Institutions and their proper and legitimate functioning is crucial for the government to formulate implement, monitor and evaluate policies for its citizens.

2. *Process: Policy as a Political Activity*

The process aspect of Public Policy Model explains the policy formulation, policy approval / authorization, implementation, monitoring and evaluation is the exclusive responsibility of the government but not limited to the government functionaries alone. The individuals and groups members of the civil society, professionals and interest groups, media as a vibrant organ of society, NGOs, CBOs and above all the political parties are all partners and stake holders in the policy process.

The situation analysis needs to be done for problem identification which demands government resources and need government action for policy cycle. Once the situation analysis is done in such a way that major problems have been identified and consensus developed then the next step is to formulate policy which means how to address / identify issues and which would be the best way to legalize the policy and who and how the policy be implemented? But before the implementation is started a policy needs to be formulated on the basis of identified problems and issues.

The question arises here that who formulates the policy. It varies from country to country and state to state. In the case of Pakistan the main responsibility of policy formulation rests with the administrative ministry which means for example, that environment policy at the national level would be drafted by the Ministry of Environment which sets the key areas for policy development. This is a common practice but in few cases it deviates from this principal. As an example the formulation of defence policy is the responsibility of the Ministry of Defence but in actual practice (defacto) the armed forces of Pakistan make this policy. Same situation, more or less, prevails in the case of Pakistan foreign policy and specially its component of Kashmir policy which is formulated by the Armed forces. There could be few other examples which can be quoted in this regard. But the administrative ministries are responsible (de jure) to formulate the policy. As long as the policy concern or policy issues are addressed in the documented policy as per identified problems then the implementation faces less serious problems. (The policy formulation has been discussed in detail Chapter 4)

What follows after the policy is formulated? It needs approval or the legitimating by the respective authority. The major responsibility of policy approval rests with the federal cabinet under the chairmanship of the Prime Minister which is the apex executive authority in the country. There are certain or short term policy stipulation which are approved / endorsed by the president or for that matter the judiciary.

Who then implements the policy? The government has the key responsibility in this regard. As a normal practice the administrative ministry or division is authorized to undertake the implementation. But this is not only limited to the ministry alone. It can seek help, assistance and support from other ministries and divisions but keeping its prime role along with coordination. The ministry of finance which holds the purse, plays equally important role in the implementation process by providing and releasing funds on regular basis. The financial crunch often hampers implementation process. But another aspect is even more crucial in this respect which is that quite often the administrative ministries don't have the technical capacity to use the available funds. Hence it is not always paucity of funds but the capacity of implementation ministry or machinery also becomes a hindrance.

Once the implementation starts the process of Monitoring and Evaluation also sets in. The monitoring is usually carried out by the administrative ministry but the over arching monitoring and evaluation responsibility has been given to the Planning Commission of the Planning and Division, Government of Pakistan. The commission is well equipped with the technical manpower to undertake this responsibility. It may not be possible for the commission to monitor and evaluate all the policies, programs and projects. About 70% of polices, programs and projects are professionally monitored and evaluated by the Planning Commission. This mechanism is primarily used for development projects financed by the government under the Public Sector Development Program (PSDP). The monitoring and evaluation of all those activities funded by the recurring budget is usually the responsibility of administrative ministry or department.

Having said that, the monitoring and evaluation exercise has also been done by different government agencies, consulting firms, individual specialists/experts, the media and press (not formal) in their own way. The monitoring and evaluation role must not be confused with the financial audit because there is separate but comprehensive arrangement prevailing under the Department of the Auditor General of Pakistan. This office is well equipped with technical staff to undertake the task of financial auditing on regular basis.

3. *Rationalism: Policy as Maximum Social Gain*

The Public Policy Model is considered very useful especially for developing countries where the development is not measured purely in economic terms. In the countries like Pakistan or take the case of South Asian region where all the countries including India are still struggling to minimize the number of people living below the poverty line. In each country this figure is staggering and runs into millions of people. Here the policies of social gain which means that Public Policy benefits large number of persons through maximum social gains. Generally the Public Policies in social sectors like Education, Health, Population Welfare, Gender and Environment exceed costs if compared to benefit ratio but provide maximum gains to greatest number of people. In the domain of Health Policy it is immensely important to minimize the number of infant mortality, child mortality and material mortality rates rather than measuring these in economic terms. It is important to know the unit cost but for development purpose and prepare budget. The avoidable deaths and diseases are more significant for a healthy society than measuring the cost of these programs in financial terms.

The two key principals often mentioned in this policy model is that no policy should be adopted if its costs exceeds its benefits and secondly decision makers should choose a policy that produces the greatest benefit over cost. Here the cost is not confined to financial cost rather it is the social cost (gains) which should be accrued over the financial cost. Healthy population, with higher literacy rate and better access to educational opportunities provide maximum social benefit to the population in the shape of organized and disciplined community, properly educated manpower for better job opportunities and healthy family structure; where the crime rate is declining and human resources are flourishing and makes the economy robust. Where the corruption and illegal gratification, use of official authority for personal financial gains and deceiving each other in daily life are all negative variants and are abhorred. However the policy formulation entrust responsibility to those who are supposed to prepare or formulate policy. Hence the policy makers need to keep in mind certain variables while focusing on 'Policy as a Maximum Social Gain' which can be summarized below.

First, there is need to know all policy options and their relative weight and outcomes. This means that how the policy would affect the target group? How many people would be affected by it positively or negatively? What would be the possibility of sustaining this policy if it is successful?

Second, the Policy makers need to be well aware of all available or most policy options. This needs empirical research with reliable and valid data, only then the policy alternatives can be measured. This is not something very difficult, because computer software can be prepared for simulation models to measure policy option, the financial cost element and policy ramification for the number of people.

Third, policy consequences are sometime serious and wide spread that it can create serious problems for the government or party in power or even for the country. The military dictator's policy in Pakistan, to accede all the demand of USA on one telephone call immediately after 9/11, 2001 has brought devastation in this country. But his dictatorship permeated with the blessings of USA. Sometime the results of certain policy options takes much longer time span but the government / political party in power gets impatient because its tenure is going to end and change the policy in wrong direction with hope to demonstrate or achieve some results.

There are certain policies which have been strangulated by the government without any valid reason. One such example is the policy of Nai Roshni Schools which was started in the late 1980s in Pakistan and was meant to provide educational opportunities for primary level education in the afternoon through condensed course of two years instead of five years. The evaluation was undertaken after two years which revealed that the policy success rate was more than 80%. This was measured against certain indicators which included school enrollment, teacher's presence, teaching-learning resources, interest of community where school was located and a dominant sign board with the name of school. All these indicators provided overwhelming positive response. However soon after this evaluation the policy was abandoned or strangulated by the then government without any known reason.

Fourth, the cost element of policy is important. But it is not only the financial cost because the social sector policies cannot be properly measured and appreciated on the basis of ratio of benefits to cost. However each policy option needs to be estimated financially for the purpose of feasibility and practicability.

Fifth, here lies the test of decision makers about the policy alternatives. The most efficient policy alternative needs to be identified, thoroughly discussed with stakeholders for modifications and changes if required to ensure the availability of funds and above all political consensus and commitment. The predictive capacity to foresee accurately the consequences of alternate policies and the intelligent financial calculations requires a decision making system that facilitates rationality in policy formulation.

4. *Incrementalism: Policy as variations on the past*

This is the most popular yet conservative model of public policy. It involves very little risks, fewer chances of failure but not bringing any substantial change in the lives of people or the target group as a result of such policy. Its popularity rests on two assumptions. First the policy makers consider this risk free, accept the legitimacy of established programs and tacitly agree to continue previous policies. Second, the uncertainty and the consequences of new or different policy cannot be fully predicted hence it is considered a safe approach to continue the ongoing policy with only certain modifications by increasing some targets.

For example in Pakistan every Education Policy eagerly mentions about the increase in the number of education institutions especially at primary level. This does not involve risk but it has deteriorated the primary education to be abysmal. The inefficient and badly managed primary education system has not improved but this failing system is expanded at a large scale.

This model of public policy is a continuation of past government activities with only incremental modifications. This approach prevents the policy/decision makers from identifying the full range of policy alternatives and their consequences. Also the time constraint, non-availability of reliable and valid data and increased cost, provides cushion and safe approach to formulate policy. The conservative part of this policy model is mostly "no pain no gain".

There is very little possibility of radical policy innovation in this model and avoid major policy shifts which involve great gains or losses and keep the policy decision to the extent where minimal risk is involved. Within this model the 'new' policy is close to current policies with possibility of meager growth and no development. The development requires innovation and change which involves greater risk of enhanced cost and uncertain successful results. The success is provided by the government ruling party and serving bureaucrats which is visible and becomes tangible during the tenure of the government. This rarely happens in a span of four/five years, which is usually the tenure of the government. When the innovation and changes are made the gestation period is usually longer depending upon the policy. In the softer programs such as education even the primary education cycle is of five years, if the building is available, trained teachers are appointed curricular and text books are prepared before the start of the academic session. But situation may be different in the policy focusing on hardware. As an example it would be quite possible to build a small factory to produce boxes within a year or so. The building would be visible to demonstrate to success of particular policy interventions but it would be capital intensive for which the huge amount of financial resources are required during the short period of four/five years. In the developing or wavering economies riddled with corruption and bad governance and kickbacks as is the case in Pakistan the decision makers would not favour such a policy option, project or program.

There is a classic example of polio vaccine with reference to Pakistan. Every year million of US dollars are spent on the import of polio vaccine. This is not a onetime expenditure because the polio vaccine is required for every new born child up to the age of five years. But no pharmaceutical company or any factory / industry in the government control produce polio vaccine locally which is quite possible as is being done in the neighboring country. Why not Pakistan Government or the Ministry/ies responsible to provide vaccine undertake this initiative? There are possibly two reasons. One, there is greater margin of kickbacks, corruption or pilferage in the import of millions of polio vaccine doses. Second there is a fear of failure because of adulteration in the manufacturing process resulting in the production of spurious drugs. Hence it is safe to import polio vaccine, though expensive, but requesting the UN agencies and other donors (UNICEF, WHO) or begging from rich countries like USA, European States etc. for the purchase of vaccine. The begging is risk free but the manufacturing is full of risks, time consuming and need resources. Every government in Pakistan has shown greater inclination of begging from rich countries but the government which comes to power in 2008 has surpassed the entire previous regime in begging.

In Support of incrementalism

The functionaries, officer or officials, working in public sector bureaucratic set up are conservative in their approach towards practical manifestations. This is not limited to any specific country, system or region. The primary reason for this behavioral dimension is that the propensity to stay away from risk, move on the familiar path and create no disagreement is safe bet. Thus the incremental model of public policy is easy to follow and minimize uncertainty. "Incrementalism is thus more satisfactory from a theoretical point of view as it scores high on criteria like coherence and simplicity"[2]. We tend to find a way which may not be the best one but which is familiar and easy to work with hence the incremental model fits well in this frame. Another aspect is to create agreement during the process of policy formulation, implementation and evaluation. The easy way to manage this process is to increase the targets and plan for enhanced budget. The budget availability, most likely, would be deficient than the estimated amount. This means that the targets would not be achieved but can easily be reasoned because of the financial resource constraint. This is quite acceptable excuse for all the stakeholders both in government and opposition. The issue of legitimacy is also important. The present policy has already been approved by the competent authority hence the enhancement of targets and demand for more budget would not generate any new debate about its legitimacy. The test of a good decision is agreement than goal achievement. This would reduce possible political tension and maintain stability.

5. *Group Theory: Policy as Group Equilibrium*

Politics is the name of possibilities and each interest group, political party, think tank and all other organizations of this nature play a pivotal role in the Group Theory Model of Public Policy. Each group make efforts to influence the political party in power and government of the day, to formulate, such policy which mostly benefit a particularly group. As an example the public sector (government) in Pakistan has miserably failed to provide access to education to the specific age group at all levels of education i.e. primary, secondary, higher secondary and higher education. The private sector as a group organized and mobilized itself to provide education facilities to the people at much expensive cost as compared to government. But they, in most cases, ensure quality of education in the private sector institutions. This group of private educational institutions has influenced the government in such a way

that it is very easy to establish school, college or even a
university in a rented house in Pakistan. However the
Higher Education Commission has laid down certain
criterion to establish a university but it could not be
implemented as planned. There is a tax holiday for the
private education institutions, their accounts cannot be
audited by the government and cannot be inspected by the
state machinery. Further the government has slided down
about the education of masses. Although there is provision
in the Constitution of Pakistan to provide free and
compulsory education up to secondary level by the state but
it remains an elusive dream and confined as rhetoric. Some
of private school systems have become cartels and are
intensively spread all over the country and few have even
expanded their wings in other countries. Here the
government has failed in its responsibility, because poor
public policy of education but more so, under the pressure
of interest groups. There are several interest groups existing
in different countries, follow their agendas, influence the
government and it may lead to group conflict. One example
is the taxation policy. Big business groups are not only
involved in tax evasion but also influence government
policy not to tax the product of that particular group. The
case in point is the land lords in Pakistan with large land-
holdings who never allowed any government to tax
agriculture sector in an agrarian economy like Pakistan. If
some strict policy stipulations for agriculture sector are
implemented, this possibility may lead to group conflicts
hence the responsibility of political system and government
is to manage group conflicts by "1)-Establishing the rules

of the game in the groups struggle 2)-Arranging compromises and balancing interests 3)-Enacting compromises in the form of Public Policy and 4)-Enforcing these compromises".[3] There could be clash of interest between industrialist, business persons and the landed aristocracy about the taxation policy. There could be strong divergent of interest between small manufacturer and large manufacturer about the taxation policy.

There is a caveat in doing this by the government. The question is how to measure or determine the influence or strength of each group. It is a complex exercise but the identified variables for this activity are 1) Number of people in the group 2) Financial status and source of income 3) Organizational strength and management capacity 4) Leadership strength and its quality 5) Access to decision makers and finally the 6) Working of group for internal cohesion. There is a note of caution here for the government that no single group should wield so much power that it overshadows or dominates the government decision making authority.

The key responsibility of a successful political system which helps to maintain equilibrium by preventing anyone group from moving too far from prevailing value. The Real Estate sector in Pakistan is good example. The 'Baharia Town' a corporate entity within the real estate has overwhelmed and in certain situation dominated the government / state institutions. There has been no gestation on the part of this private entity to massively influence and in certain situation control executive, legislatures or even judiciary. It seems "what may be called public policy is actually the equilibrium reached in the group struggle at any given moment, and it represents a balance which the contending factors or groups constantly strive to trip in their favor. The legislature referees the group struggle, ratifies the victories of successful coalition and record the terms of surrenders, compromises and conquests in the form of statutes" [4]

Sometime situation so arises that certain individuals who belong to anyone group also belong to another group. This creates a dichotomy where the balance has to be created to moderate the influence of both sides.

6. *Elite Theory: Policy as Elite Preference*

Theoretically and even logically the Public Policy preferences and provision must emanate from the needs and demands of masses. But in reality it remains a myth. In the Elite theory model, the values and preference of governing elite determines the basic structure and subsequently formulation of Public Policy. What usually happens is that elite actually shape mass opinion where as it should have been the other way around.

Hence the elite share consensus rather dominates the basic values of social system and preservation of the system. It is known that countries or societies do not have equality in the social and economic system. There are dirty rich, rich, middle class, poor and very poor which manifests the inequality. But the redeeming features of organized societies are that each and every group rich or poor is equal before law. The principle of equality in the domain of rule of law is predetermined.

The elite theory model by implication and practice pre-supposes or views masses as largely passive, apathetic and ill informed, mass sentiments are often manipulated by elites. The communication between elites and masses flow downward. Thus the Elite theory can be summarized briefly as follows:

1. "Society is divided into the few who have power and many who don't only a smaller number of persons allocate values for society; the masses do not decide public policy.

2. The few who govern are not typical of the masses that are governed. Elites are drawn disproportionately from the upper Socio-Economic strata of Society.

3. The movement of non-elites to elite positions must be slow and continuous to maintain stability and avoid revolution. Only non-elites who have accepted the basic elite consensus can be admitted to governing circles.

4. Public policy does not reflect the demands of masses but rather the prevailing values of the elite. Changes in public policy will be incremental rather than revolutionary.

5. Active elites are subject to relatively little direct influence from apathetic masses. Elite influence masses more than masses influence elites." [5]

Having said all that it does not mean that there is no competition among elites or they do not have different preferences or opinions. But the differences are very narrow on the multiple issues hence the elite agree more often than they disagree.

7. Public Choice Theory: Policy as Collective Decision Made by Self-Interested Individuals

There are two underlying assumptions in the realm of Public Choice Theory. First, individuals act in politics in the same way as they interact in market place to protect their economic interests. Hence it establishes a closer relationship and link between the study of Economics and Political Science. It is a matter of general observation that the study of economics focuses to understand the behavior in the market place and individuals pursued their private economic interests. This is done primarily to actualize their economic needs but also to understand and influence market forces for individual benefit. The discipline of political science studied behavior in the public arena and assumed that individuals pursued their own notion of public interest. The model assumes that the individuals struggle to seek and maximize their personal benefits in politics as well as market places. The commonality in Politics and Economics is to protect the self-interests and pursue personal benefits.

Second that the government must perform certain functions that the market place is unable to handle; that is, it must remedy certain "market factures". The manifestation of this component is that public choice theory must ensure and provide those public goods and services by the government where the costs exceed their values to any single buyers and a single buyer would not be in a position to keep non-buyers from using it. One common example is that National defense is meant to protect the individuals and state from foreign invasion which is too expensive for a single person to buy and once it is provided no one can be excluded from its benefits. Another aspect is the externalities to market forces which cause failure in public policy by pursuing individual benefit. The air and water pollution imposes uncompensated costs on others. Here the government either regulates those externalities or impose penalties on those activities to compensate for their costs to society.

As a consequence what can be said is that the role of government becomes vital in the Model of Public Choice Theory. First because most or all the "Political actors, voters, taxpayers, candidates, legislature, bureaucrats, interest groups, parties, bureaucracies and government seek to maximize their personal benefit in politics as well as market place". But who is going to protect the life, property, rights etc. of individuals? It is the government and state to undertake this responsibility. Secondly Public Choice Theory explains why political parties and candidates generally fail to provide policy alternatives?

8. Game Theory: Policy as a Rational Choice in Competitive Situation

The term 'game' is used in this model in the context of dependent variable which means that policy action in one situation may not yield the same results if the setting or stage is modified or changed. Hence the 'players' of the 'game' must "adjust their conduct to reflect not only their own desires and abilities but also their expectations about what others will do"[6]. This theory or concept is often used in international conflicts or conflict resolutions.

The model can also be distantly compared with the operational research. "Operational research is the application of the methods of science to complete problems arising in the direction and management of large systems of men, machines, materials and money in industry, business, government and defence. The distinctive approach is to develop a scientific model of the system, incorporating measurements of factors such as chance and risk, with which to predict and compare the outcomes of alternative decisions, strategies or control. The purpose is to help management determine its policy and actions scientifically"[7]. The key element of this research requires that, what would be the effect on the output and outcome of a given input. If we need to substantiate the model then it can be said that if a boundary wall is built in girls primary school in rural area in a country like Pakistan, the girl enrollment would increase. Similarly the facility of drinking water would enhance enrollment of girls. In the context of boundary wall it is presumed that it would provide security to the girl students and also 'Purdah' would be observed. The availability of drinking water particularly in the summer would not only be considered a blessing but genuinely support the needs of human body for enough liquid to be maintained in the hot weather. How much enrollment would be increased with each of these interventions is a question which can be asked or expected from the results of operation research. However there is little or no game element hence in these circumstances, other than the conflict situation, it is a misnomer to call it a game theory.

A popular example is given of the game of 'chicken' in the context of this model. "Two adolescents drive their cars towards each other at a high speed, each with one set of wheels on the center line of the highway. If nether veers off course they will crash. Whoever veers is "chicken". Both drivers prefer to avoid death, but they also want to avoid the "dishonor" of being "chicken". The outcome depends of what both drivers do, and each driver must try to predict how the other will behave. The form of "brinkmanship" is common in international relations"[8].

It would be better for both drivers to veer so that the crash would be avoided but it would be the value judgment of each driver how he perceives dishonor vis-à-vis death. If dishonor is placed at a high value pedestal than the possibility to veer minimizes and raises greater chances of crash to be followed by the likelihood of death.

However the real utility of game theory seems more in the conflict situations where the policymaking options are discussed.

References

[1] Saleem; Farrukh: The NEWS International: Lahore: March 10, 2013: p

[2] Jane-Erik Lave: The Public Sector, London: Sage: 2000: p75

[3] Dye, T.R: Understanding Public Policy: New Jersey, 2002, page 21.

[4] Earl Latham "The Group Basis of Politics", in Political Behaviour ed. Heinz Eulan San, Elders veld aid Morris Janowitz (New York, Free Press, 1956) p239.

[5] Thomas R. Dye: Understanding Public Policy, upper Saddle River, New Jersey: 2002: p23&24

[6] Thomas R. Dye: Understanding Public Policy, upper Saddle River, New Jersey: 2002: p27

[7] The UK's Operational Research Society had defined this term. It has been Quted in T.A.Burley and G.O.Sullivan: Operational Research, London: Macmillan.1986: p2

[8] Thomas R. Dye: Understanding Public Policy, upper Saddle River, New Jersey: 2002: p28

3

POLICY FORMULATION

Is it inevitable?

T here are several reasons to undertake this endeavor of formulation exercise but three reasons are tangible for overall comprehension of public policy.

First: The designing of public policy or the formulation of Public Policy follows different steps and approaches before a policy is formulated. Policies are formed in different situations by different governments/ruling elites at different times with different objectives and strategies. It becomes necessary for the incumbent government and the individual entrusted with the task of formulating public policy, to look at all the different aspects and situations when the policy is formulated, implemented and evaluated. It provides guidance as what to do and what not to do on the basis of experience, comparison and analysis. Both the positive and negative aspects provide guidance and lessons for the future policy formulation. In certain situation there are hidden assumptions in policy development especially in foreign and defense policies in most of the countries and more so in the countries, like Pakistan.

Second: The development of policy process is essentially a political activity because the public policy is based upon those guidelines which have been provided by the Politician. Also the final policy approval is given by the politicians in power. However this process cannot be completed unless the policy substance, data, reports analysis, opinion and choices of people at large and the bureaucratic setup gives important information. This support mechanism enables the completion of policy process professionally. However there is word of caution here that public policy preparation is also a technical exercise which must need the support and guidance of professional persons. It cannot be left to the politicians alone because their vision of policy goes up to and not beyond next elections. Whereas policy of any sector and of any government usually is a long term commitment which needs continuous help of professionals in their respective fields to stay on course and bureaucracy which has the key responsibility to implement and yield results as envisaged in the objectives.

Three: The success or failure of policy implementation is closely linked to the policy formulation process. How? If the policy is formulated based on reliable data and valid assumptions; the ground realities have been understood in proper perceptive; the persons responsible to implement the policy have been involved in the policy formulation and the policy beneficiaries have also been the partners in the process of policy development, all these factors would result in the formulation of sound policy. These are the minimum requirements to understand this phase of public policy. We can conclude and stand firm that policy formulation is a very serious activity on which depends the future of millions of people and sometime it effects (positively or negatively), and go beyond one generation.

Here is a model, suggestive as it is, to help in the preparation of policy, which can be called a **Six step Model**.

Figure - 3

Policy Formulation Six Step Model

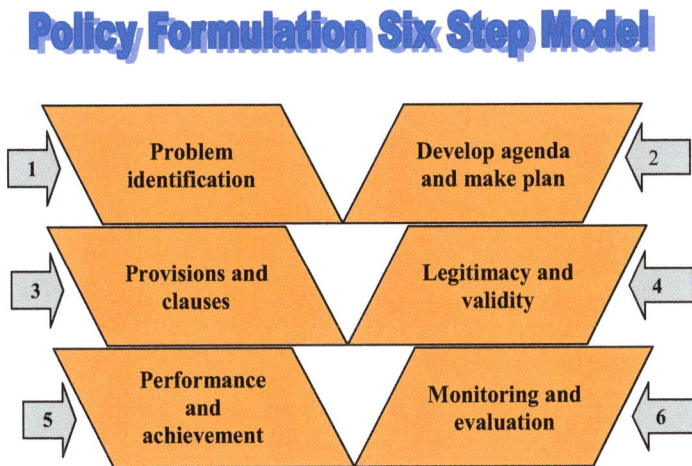

1	Problem identification	Develop agenda and make plan	2
3	Provisions and clauses	Legitimacy and validity	4
5	Performance and achievement	Monitoring and evaluation	6

1. *Situation Analysis and Problem Identification*

In any country, developed or developing, the problem identification is a complex and difficult activity. The problems, prima facia, are multifarious. The individuals, interest groups, political parties and government machinery perceive problems in their own respective surroundings. The perceptions are important but what is critical are the facts and realities on the ground. Each operating policy anywhere has certain strengths as well as weaknesses. During the time of problem identification the situation analysis should be done in such a way that both strengths and weaknesses of existing policies are kept in proper perceptive without exaggeration either negatively or positively. One of the most useful methods generally used for this purpose is SWOT analysis. It is scientific techniques and follows a step by step approach. It is considered a standard way of understanding, comprehending and analyzing the (S) Strengths, (W) Weaknesses, (O) Opportunities and (T) Threats. The strengths and weaknesses relate to the existing performance of the organization but opportunities and threats are weighed in the future context.[1]

However the main responsibility for SWOT analysis rests with the incumbent government or the political party in power to identify problems in such a way that properly address the party manifesto and juxtapose the ground realities for viable solutions to implement different options. As an example there has been confusion and uncertainty about the poverty figures in Pakistan that how many numbers of people are living below the poverty line in the country. However this anomaly of statistics / poverty figures is not limited to Pakistan. This problem is acute in developing countries but the developed countries are not free from this confusion. What happens, generally, is that the government / political party in power depress the poverty figures and inflate economic achievements.

Whereas the opposition takes a diametrically opposite stance to inflate poverty figures and depresses economic achievements. Both these approaches are irrational hence incorrect. This creates confusion and misguides the government to properly identify problems. It is not something very difficult to agree on a definition of poverty. The poverty definitions are internationally accepted all over the world. It could be person earning one US dollar a day or less or a person taking less than 2500 calories per day are considered to be the one living below the poverty line. According to these definitions comparative poverty figures are as follows[2]:

Table – 6: Poverty in South Asian Countries

Country	Total Population (Millions)	% Population below International poverty line of US$ 1.25 per day
Bangladesh	162.22	50
Bhutan	6.97	26
India	1198.00	42
Maldives	3.09	N.A
Nepal	29.33	55
Pakistan	180.80	23
Sri Lanka	20.23	14

Source: These figures have been lifted from the State of World Children Report 2011.

The official poverty figures in Pakistan is 25% but some independent estimate, suggest the poverty figures is about 40%. It is necessary that correct poverty figures must be known for problem identification. "The economic statistics have been doctored and defaced to the extent which has never been witnessed before. The budget (2010-2011) has been financed by printing notes by the State Bank of Pakistan at a scale never witnessed in the economic history of the country"[3].

There is a standard and recognized way to measure poverty in different counties. But in Pakistan "poverty is measured on the basis of Household Income Expenditure Survey conducted by the Pakistan Bureau of Statistics"[4].

It looks quite mysterious that Government has failed to release the data set of survey because someone will estimate the poverty figures correctly and ahead of Government. The government released the figures that people living below the poverty line has declined from 17.2% (nobody believes this figure) in 2007-08 to slightly above 12% (nobody believes this figure) in 2010-11. In other words in three years time seven million people have been brought out of poverty. "Given the economic conditions that have prevailed over the last three years, finding such a reduction in poverty flouts established economic theory"[5].

There are certain activities which need to be carried out in the problem identification phase which include highlighting the problems of society, expressing demands for government action, and above all is the WILL of Society which is inclusive of government, to identify genuine problems of people. The role of public opinion needs to be publicized through media, (Electronic, Print, and Social) in the formation and active participation of interest groups of citizen and collective efforts of stakeholders for a meaningful collaboration.

2. Develop agenda and make plans

In the existing literature of Public Policy a considerable amount of research has been done and still in progress on the importance and necessity of agenda setting. However there are still closed fields such as defence, foreign affairs and science policy. But the situation varies from country to country. One common feature is that the Ministry/ Department/ Persons responsible for agenda setting discuss and examine the validity of some strategies for undertaking an active search for issues rather than relying on issues to emerge. Some of the strategies in this context are[6]:

i)   Anticipating problems and opportunities despite the fact that there is time, technical and knowledge constraints.

ii) Identifying problems even where there are only weak signals. Such identification will help prepare to understand emergence of future problems. Even limited knowledge will not preclude fuller investigation later.

iii) There remains the need to rectify unequal access to the policy agenda. Rectification of such inequality of access may depend on one's perception of that inequality. The generation and use of empirical research can best be used for mitigating this problem.

Agenda setting for a public policy is a complex activity because the interest groups (Political, Business, Media) would influence the government or the people in power to advance their interests to be reflected in the policy formulation. This is not entirely negative but it usually is done at the expense of masses or people who are marginalized financially, socially and politically. If this happens the agenda setting would be misdirected and create more problems than addressing the issues of poverty, health, education, clean water, roads, electricity, power generation etc. A pro-active role has to be played not only by Civil Society but also the mass media, political parties' public officials and legislatures so that the policy agenda must address the real issues and benefit major segment of society and not elite few.

3. *Provision and Clauses*

Public Policy Formulation in social sector is essentially an exercise to formulate policy proposals to resolve issues and mitigate the problems of people. Apparently it seems simple or less complex but there is a fear and note of caution that policy formulation should not deviate from agreed agenda which reflect the needs and problems of people. Political parties have their manifestos and they need to mention those clauses in the policy document. This is for two reasons. First it would reflect the commitment of political parties to resolve people's problem and secondly the electorate would also be involved in the policy formulation not only as beneficiaries but also as political and social partners. Before devising and formulating policy it is important that policy appraisal is undertaken. There is usually a debate what is the essential difference between appraisal and evaluation. Appraisal is undertaken when potential policies are being assessed but the evaluation is done when the existing policies are being assessed. It is a common demand and also a practice in several countries to undertake a thorough appraisal before policy is finalized continued or modified.

"Policy appraisal is the process of considering the feasibility of policy proposal, presumably before a final decision is made. Such appraisals are more likely to correlate to more 'rational' approaches to policymaking. In the terminology of the cyclical or process model, evaluation occurs after implementation of a policy"[7].

4. *Legitimacy and Validity*

Policy only becomes public policy when it is legitimized with the approval of legislative body. Before it goes to the legislative body (National Assembly in the case of Pakistan) for Enactment; the policy is sent to select committee of the National Assembly or parliament relevant to the subject policy. Here the policy provisions are discussed thoroughly by the representative of different political parties and then sent to the cabinet with recommended changes / modifications. If the cabinet approves the changes it goes to the legislature for enactment by simple majority vote. If the changes proposed by Select Committee are not approved by the cabinet then it goes to the relevant ministry for policy modification so that a revised version of the policy is sent to cabinet.

The political support for enacting a policy into an Act of Parliament is necessary. It also means to get the support of the electorate for the selection of policy proposals. The policy legislation is primarily a decision about its constitutionality that extends legitimating for implementation by the government and other stakeholders. Some time the decisions of the superior judiciary are also sought for legitimating purposes.

It happens, not often, that a certain policy is legitimate but not valid as per the social and cultural norms of a society or country. On the other hand certain policies and practices are considered valid but not legitimate. One such example is that of child marriage and child labor, in Pakistan and also in other developing countries particularly south Asia. Similarly circumcisne of female in Africa used to be valid practice but not legitimate. Even with legislative backing to stop it the practice still continues in some of the African countries.

5. *Performance and achievement*

Public policy implementation requires government structure, legal sanctions, financial resources and executive authority. The most important of these elements is the finances. Now where it comes from? It is provided by the tax payers. The taxation policy and tax collection mechanism remains the prerogative of government. The government has the authority to formulate tax laws, implement those laws and provide resources and authority to achieve policy targets.

The public policy can neither be treated as theoretical exercise nor only as an intellectual or academic preposition. It is a deliberate effort to formulate policy to achieve tangible results in a given time span and allocated resources. However there is always a possibility to do the course correction, if required, and modify time line based on the monitoring report. The question has been raised quite often by the students of public administration with special focus on public policy as how to precisely measure the quality provisions / aspects of policy objective. This concern is valid and important. There are no easy ways to do it. One such example is how to measure the quality of life of people? It requires concerted effort to do that, for which key performance indicators (KPIs) have to be developed with the help of Monitoring and Evaluation specialists.

The thrust of the argument is that policy formulation and implementation is expected to achieve some definitive results which could be quantitative or qualitative or both.

6. *Monitoring and Evaluation*

Monitoring and evaluation are important sources of feedback to the entire process of planning. Performance appraisal at the planning level has its particular relevance, by feeding information on the realistic implementation of plans, programmes and projects to other hierarchies and management system. Monitoring and supervision as essential components for tracking the progress are being given new orientations, especially at the micro-level.

Whenever any policy comes into operation there arises the need for some kind of mechanism by which the progress of implementation can be readily assessed. Such a mechanism is generally referred to as the monitoring mechanism. Generally, monitoring covers activities of inspection and supervision. Inspection has been common practice for monitoring. Today, many countries avoid the use of the term inspection because it carries with it very hierarchical, authoritative and evaluative-cum-directional connotations. These are not readily compatible with increasingly decentralized and participatory developmental systems.

Difference between Monitoring & Evaluation

There is an overlap between the two terms because both are management and planning tools. Similarly, several definitions can be devised for both these concepts. The first major difference is that monitoring is done against the identified activities of the policy. But the evaluation focuses more on the objectives of the same policy. The second difference is that monitoring is an on-going and constant activity whereas evaluation is periodic, to be done and completed within a specific time. Thirdly, monitoring is generally considered and practiced as an internal component of the administrative Ministry. But this does not mean that monitoring cannot be done externally. But evaluation is both internal and external.

The monitoring and evaluation is a systematic procedure to collect and analyze information about the policy implementation. The monitoring measures the effectiveness of planning and management periodically. The purpose of monitoring is to provide timely information and give feedback to the management on vital stages in implementation. The monitoring is a concurrent activity associated with every stage of the implementation. The periodic feedback on the progress helps management to know the achievement vis-a-vis targets. It helps the management to take appropriate steps for proper implementation. It can correct wagging time-schedule, synchronization of related activities and identify the gaps in various components of implementation. It is a system of forewarning the deviation from its chartered or targeted course.

Pragmatic planning involves the realistic assessment of financial resources and other required inputs that can be expended on development activities each year and during the implementation of policy appraisal. On the assumption of the technical feasibility tells us about the viability and the impact of the proposed investment.

Policy Formulation in Pakistan

Public policy making in Pakistan has been based on an informal approach hence every ministry evolves its own methodology to develop a policy document. There has been a lack of understanding about the importance of public policy which is clearly manifest that a non serious approach is adopted for this activity. There are major steps in the policy process right from the beginning to the end of formulation mechanism. As an example the Health policy formulation in Pakistan prima facia adopted following steps:

Figure - 4

Policy Formulation in Pakistan: Eight Steps

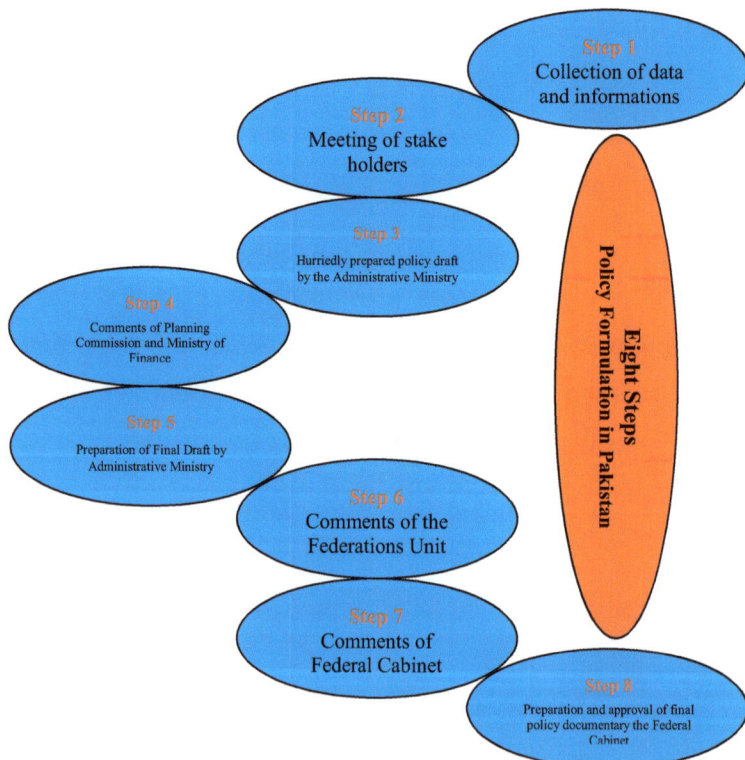

Step 1 — Collection of data and informations

Step 2 — Meeting of stake holders

Step 3 — Hurriedly prepared policy draft by the Administrative Ministry

Step 4 — Comments of Planning Commission and Ministry of Finance

Step 5 — Preparation of Final Draft by Administrative Ministry

Step 6 — Comments of the Federations Unit

Step 7 — Comments of Federal Cabinet

Step 8 — Preparation and approval of final policy documentary the Federal Cabinet

Policy Formulation in Pakistan — Eight Steps

Step I:- *Collection   of   data   and   Information:*
Information is collected by the Ministry of Health,
Government of Pakistan from Bio statistics unit and Health
Management Information System (HMIS). There are other
channels to obtain information some of which include
survey reports, national census, research studies, evaluation
reports etc. The relevant record is also researched to
unearth such information which has been collected earlier
but neither used nor analyzed. These include several
evaluation studies undertaken by the project wing of the
planning commission. Many reports have been prepared by
the International donors (UN agencies) and lending
agencies (World Bank, Asian Development Bank) based on
third party evaluation and independent researches.

Step II:-*Meeting of Stakeholders:* Meetings are held
between and among the representatives of the federal
(ministries) and provincial departments of Health, Planning
and other stakeholders. Key areas/issues are identified and
some options to address these areas are discussed with
minimal participation of people's representatives / NGOs.
Some consensus is developed so that the process of policy
making proceeds. The quality of these meetings are quite
ordinary and often do not meet the minimum requirements
for this endeavor. For example meetings are held as routine
practice often without agenda and poor participation of
stakeholders. There is no ownership of the output of these
meetings.

Step III:-*Hurriedly prepared policy draft by the
Administrative Ministry:* The officers of the Ministry of

Health hurriedly prepare draft which is known as a first draft or preliminary draft. This draft is further improved with the help of some informal discussion with other officers of the different ministries for which there has been no scientific method and organized way to record the key issues and mitigation strategies. However some record occasionally is kept as the proceedings of the meeting. There is a minimal practice of using reliable and valid information. The focus of these meetings is to setup quantitative targets without giving any review or consideration how these could be achieved. The easy way adopted is to follow the linear projection model thus increase the number of Basic Health Units (BHU), Rural Health Centers (RHS), Dispensers, Doctors and Medical staff. The service delivery and the quality of services remain at the periphery.

Step IV:-Comments of Planning Commission and Ministry of Finance: This revised draft is sent to the Planning Commission and the Ministry of Finance separately for their views. The planning commission discusses this draft in the context of overall National Policy formulation process and undertakes the policy appraisal and feasibility to measure the potential of the success / achievement of the proposed draft. The Finance Ministry gives a serious thought about the financial implications, resource generation, allocation of funds and its utilization. The feedback from the planning commission and Finance Ministry is discussed again at the Health Ministry and the core group of provincial representatives to further shapeup the policy document. After some deliberations a final draft is prepared by the Ministry of Health for the approval of the Federal Cabinet.

Step V:-Preparation of Final Draft by Administrative Ministry: The Federal Cabinet has the prerogative to either accept it as it is or suggest certain modifications and improvements on the basis of the observations and suggestion. The policy document goes back to Ministry of Health for revision under the guidelines of the Federal Cabinet. Simultaneously the policy document is also shared with the Provincial Governments more for the purposes of consensus building and legitimacy rather than to bring any substantive changes. But some policy provisions can be changed if any strong point of view comes from the provinces.

Step VI:-Comments of the Federating Unit: A final policy document is prepared by the Ministry of Health and submitted to the Federal Cabinet for approval. Once it is approved by the cabinet then it becomes a formal National Policy. This document is presented to the National Assembly more for information than for approval. This final document becomes the guiding principle for the preparation of the Five Year Development Plan. The Planning Commission plays a leading role in the development of the Plan which becomes the basis of project development process. The federal and provincial Health Ministries prepare projects so that composite Public Sector Development Programme (PSDP) is prepared. The funds are allocated to the new as well on going projects depending upon the satisfactory performance of the ongoing projects.

Step VII*:-*Comments of Federal Cabinet: The project implementation is in part the reflection of policy implementation in smaller segments. The different policy objectives and key policy programmes are developed into project cycle and the respective administrative ministries and departments implement the approved projects.

Step VIII*:-*Preparation and approval of final policy document by the Federal Cabinet: The Monitoring and Evaluation (M&E) of Projects is done by the respective ministries which are usually the agencies implementing the project. But more regular and rigorous exercise of M&E is done by the Planning Commission which is well equipped to undertake this responsibility. Similarly the Planning Commission also undertakes the task of Monitoring & Evaluation of the policy and it is presented to the Deputy Chairperson of the Planning Commission who briefs the Cabinet about the progress of policy implementation.

References

[1] For more details on SWOT analysis; Khawaja, Sarfraz: Good Governance and Result Based Monitoring: Islamabad: Poorab Academy: 2011

[2] The State of the World's Children 2011: UNICEF: United Nations Children Fund: February 2011: New York: p112-114

[3] Dr. Muhammad Yaqub: Article "What to expect in the next Budget 2011-2012": The News International, Islamabad: May 8, 2012: p6.

[4] Dr. Ashfaque H. Khan: "Poverty number revised": The News International, Islamabad: May 8, 2012: p6

[5] Dr. Ashfaque H. Khan

[6] Hogwood, B.W and L.A. Gunn: Policy Analysis for the real World: Oxford: Oxford University Press: 1984: p69-72

[7] Allama Iqbal Open University, Islamabad: Commonwealth of Learning Executive MBA/MPA: Sc1 Public Policy, Code 5572: 2004: p60

4

POLICY
IMPLEMENTATION
Why so Many Hiccups?

Introduction

T he Public Policy Implementation is one of the most crucial phases of policy cycle. Generally policy implementation has been left to the bureaucratic setup which may not be in a position (capacity, finances, manpower, and technical support) to gainfully and effectively implement the policy. The policy must be applied in the real world situation and ground realities but this aspect which is known as 'implementation' is often overlooked. The detailed plan of action, realistic as it needs to be, is often missing or haphazardly prepared. Hence the lack of well thought out plan of action does not provide guidance for efficient and effective implementation. It has often been observed and experienced that the policy implementation is left to loyal (to the boss), dedicated (self interest) and disinterested career administrators.

Implementation

The policy makers either do not fully comprehend the problems of implementation or more likely they choose not to understand the pitfalls of policy implementation. When policy filters through different ministries and departments for implementation, it is not understood in such a way that the stakeholders (ministries / department) are on the same lines. This creates a serious conceptual problem because policy making, under the best circumstances, is a hypothetical experiment without explaining or enumerating any Implementation Plan or Plan of Action.

Generally policy is based on unexamined conventional wisdom, individual biases of bureaucratic hierarchy, involving construction of casual model (Implicit or Explicit), opinion (often erroneous), guess work, misconceptions and above all lack of research carried out scientifically.

In retrospect, while looking at the policy implementation, there are four scenarios which emerge for the purpose of Policy Analysis. First, Policy was sound but implementation was poor. Second policy was sound and so was the implementation hence policy was rated as success. Third, policy was bad but implementation under the given circumstances was good which resulted into a limited success. Fourth, policy was bad and so was the implementation and the result was comprehensive failure.

There is a need to identify variables which can be termed for sound policy characteristics and then key elements of good (effective) implementation of a policy. Following are the Sound Policy Characteristics:

1) Availability, collection and use of valid and reliable information which has been used in policy preparation.

2) Planning based on realistic assumptions taking full cognizance of ground realities.

3) Active participation of key stakeholders and involvement of focused groups and expected beneficiaries.

4) Focused Policy Targets which are deliverables and measurable both quantitatively and qualitatively.

5) Avoid generalities and long list of objectives. Delineate specific objectives.

6) Avoid use of synonyms such as effects, fulfill, achieve, discharge, set in motion, do establish, accomplish, finish, realize and actualize. As and when these synonyms are used it should be followed by simple and precise meaning or explanation.

Similarly successful implemental variables of policies can be identified based on the following variables.

1) Policy document must contain an Action Plan which is clear, comprehensive and provide road map for implementation. Although policy is a long term commitment and prepared in that perspective

but the implementation plan is flexible and can be modified and fine-tuned as the policy implementation progresses.

2) The critical mass of human resources is absolutely necessary for policy implementation. This group (critical mass) must be well qualified, properly trained and possess relevant experience. This element of human resources is even more important than the financial resources. Most of the policies either lagged behind the targets or out-rightly fail not necessarily because of the financial constraints rather the non-availability of properly qualified and trained personnel or poorly trained and in experienced manpower. If the implementers are competent then they would manage the resources efficiently and use technical manpower effectively. It happens often that money is spent in huge amounts but does not achieve policy objectives.

3) The most critical component of successful implementation variables, particularly in Pakistan and generally in developing countries is good governance. This term is commonly used but frequently misunderstood as government. Governance relates to the management of all those processes that in any society define the environment which permits and enables individuals and group of individuals to raise their capability levels on the one hand, and provide opportunities

to realize their potential and enlarge the set of available choices on the other. These processes covering the political, social and economic aspects of life, impact every level of human enterprise, they cover the state, civil society and the markets, each of which is critical for sustaining human developments. There are certain distinct characteristics of Good Governance which stand on the four pillars of Accountability, participation, predictability and Transparency.[1]

Most of the countries announce policies in different sectors keeping in view, the stark national realities and put national interest at the forefront. Pakistan is neither short of policies nor policy legislation. It is the implementation which lags behind to such an extent that it distorts the development process of the country. Five Year Development Plan stipulations and program implementation has been the key to measure the success of any policy. But the implementation remained a stumbling block due to varied reasons, notwithstanding the bad governance and massive corruption. The financial corruption remained at the top of the list but the gross misuse of authority for personal gains eroded the fabric of governance.

However during the 1960s Pakistan experienced highest rates of industrial growth of 7% or more during the decade. One of the major reasons assigned to this success has been the successful implementation of Five Year Development plans, a model which was replicated even more efficiently by South Korea. As a result the economic as well as social policies of South Korea brought sustainable prosperity in the country. Whereas Pakistan abandoned consistent long term policy implementation and as a result its economic and social development lagged behind and economic growth rate moved like a pendulum and eventually declined and persists to almost 3% per annum. Pakistan is an agricultural country but its agriculture productivity contributes less than 21% to its GDP as mentioned in the Human Development report of UNDP in 2013.

The Public Policy literature since 1970 has focused on the implementation aspect whereas before that the policy formulation remained more important. As a result of these efforts two main approaches to the study of implementation have emerged. "These are the top down 'Forward Planning' approach and the bottom up 'Backward Mapping' approach. The two represent methodologies to analyze policy, as it is implemented rather to prescribe how to implement policy".[2]

1.   *Top-Down Approach*

The key proponents of this approach are Derthick[3], Pressman and Waldavsky [4] . Derthick analyzed implementation process through the study of urban policy. Whereas Pressman and Waldavsky enunciated that implementation is an ability to forge links of policy stipulation in a casual chain which usually is reflected in the different programs and projects. It is a common finding that most of the Public Policies do not achieve the stated objectives. Every ministry or department responsible for policy implementation has several reasons to mention as to why the implementation lagged behind and in certain cases remained within the cage of planning and advocacy.

In some situations even the financial resources are expended on the pretext of policy implementation but nothing tangible is delivered or achieved. One such glaring example was the construction of Kalabagh Dam in Pakistan. The total estimated cost of the Dam was US$ 3.46 billion in 1987. The implementation phase started and the residential colonies for the labourers and junior staff were constructed. Necessary manpower and technical support was put in place, transport facilities including the purchase of vehicles were acquired but the whole implementation phase was doomed in the political quagmire and it was made so controversial that the policy was abandoned to construct the Dam. If the dam is constructed now in 2013 and made operational the estimated cost would be US$ 12.3 billion. This was an example of the failure of the implementation of the top-down approach. There could be many other obstacles which can be identified as reasons for implementation failure. Some of these are:

- In most of the developing countries and few developed (Japan, Italy) countries the frequent and uncertain change of government makes the policy implementation quite difficult / challenging and in certain situation impossible.

- There is lack of identification of the agency or the Ministry which would be fully responsible for the implementation of the Public Policy. The divided responsibility means no responsibility hence no accountability and the eventual result is policy failure.

- It is not unusual that policy implementation in most of the cases involves several individuals, different government Ministries / Departments, private firms, interest groups and sometime non-government organizations. There is lack of understanding and coordination among varied stakeholders and policy execution becomes the victim of dispersed and undefined responsibility. Sometimes diarchy plays negative role. This needs to be streamlined for effective and timely implementation.

- Priority setting is a key not only in policy planning and formulation but more so in implementation. This needs the identification of the most important and critical aspects of Public Policy which need serious attention of Policy Makers so that immediate financial and other resources are made available for implementation. In the implementation of Primary Health Care policy the crucial input is the paramedic staff / doctor and medicines. But it is observed that usually it is the building (such as one/ two room as dispensary) gets the preference. The priority is the trained paramedic staff which can work without a building structure whereas a well constructed air conditioned dispensary cannot work without needed human resources.

- The resources allocation for policy implementation is dicey situation. Funds are allocated rather announced as a political rhetoric which are insufficient even for political slogans. But the availability of these funds to the responsible Ministry / Department on timely basis remained an elusive dream.

- The Economic policies (Monetary and Fiscal policies) of the incumbent government often create problems for the provision of adequate resources. The fluctuating local currency value (Rupees in the case of Pakistan), money supply, revenue collection and such situation create further hindrance in the provision and availability of adequate resources.

- Public policy can only be called or established as public policy if it is owned by the government. This ownership is the legitimating status of the policy, obtained through the enactment, cabinet decisions or approval by the administrative authority responsible for such authorization. The situation varies from country to country in this regard. This legal status has sanction of authority for allocation of resources, appointment of technical manpower and implementation follow up. This also ensures that political leadership has to take responsibility for monitoring the implementation progress of the policy. Hence the administrative setup is bound to discharge its responsibility in the context of a given policy.

- Policy legislation and resources allocation alone cannot efficiently and effectively implement the policy unless the administrative and management structure has the capacity to implement the programs and projects which emanates from policy. It has been observed in several developing countries including Pakistan where the prevailing administrative structure does not have the capacity not only to implement policy but also unable to use allocated resources specially the available funds. This mostly happens in the softer sectors. It is easy to built a school and spend money but it is time consuming and tedious to recruit and appoint qualified and experienced teachers, revise or modernize curriculum and modify evaluation system. For these items money would be available but difficult to use on timely basis to accrue success for the policy. Similarly establishment of tertiary level hospital is far less challenging than to establish primary health care units in rural areas where population is sparse and accessibility is difficult. The appointment and availability of doctors and paramedics staff would be quite a challenge for Basic Health Units in rural areas.

The top-down approach has some inherent problems in the implementation of public policy hence it becomes difficult to achieve the stated policy objectives. In more precise terms "An inquiry about implementation seeks to determine whether an organization can bring together men and materials as a cohesive organizational block and motivate them in such a way as to carry organizations stated objectives."[5]

It can be concluded that the top-down model place too much emphasis on goals or policy objectives rather than defining, streamlining and encouraging the role of different personnel responsible for performing different duties and roles. Hence the top-down model lacks effective implementation practice.

2. *Bottom-Up Approach*

The founding father of this approach is considered to be Michael Lipsky. He has suggested that the implementers of this approach can be called "Street level bureaucrats"[6]. The key focuses of this approach is that the implementers are not just Public Servants and beneficiaries of implementation but they are partners in the process hence called street level bureaucrats. It is the lower rung of the society which is the backbone of implementation in the bottom-up approach. The crux of this approach is that

i)   Public policy making is participated or prepared by those who would be responsible to implement the policy or closely associated with the implementation process.

ii)   The bottom-up approach emphasizes on consensus-building and dialogue at the time of policy preparation and formation. If that happens only then the implementation can be effective as envisaged in this approach.

iii)   The bureaucratic control over people responsible for implementation would not result into effective implementation rather it would be frequent interaction with people or their clients at the street level. This can only happen it the bureaucracy or the bureaucratic setup change the mindset of top-down approach and adapt them in a mode which has to be people friendly for successful implementation.

iv)   The expectations of people are much closer to the basics of bottom-up approach because it provides enough information and emphasis about the perception of common people. It also involves them in such a way and to a greater extent that they not only feel but also own the policy and its implementation through programs and projects.

v)   The political environment usually is a slippery preposition. It has to be properly understood by the implementers specially the bureaucrats because the people they intend to associate for bottom-up implementation are more sensitive and responsive to the political situation.

vi)   The public policy preparation is not left to the professionals alone because their perception of problems would be myopic or too academic hence the policy implementation may not achieve what was intended. Doctors to prepare health policy, teachers to develop education policy, engineers to draft engineering policy are something which is not desirable but the inputs of professionals is absolutely necessary. There is another danger that if public policy is exclusively prepared by professionals it may be skewed in favour of high tech instruments, construction of new and expensive buildings as tertiary level hospitals at the cost of primary health care system which is supposed to provide service delivery to 80% population.

3.   *Game model implementation approach*

This game model approach does not enjoy the recognition as the two above mentioned implementation approaches i.e. Top-down and Bottom-up approaches. The proponent or the advocate of this approach was Bardach[7] who advanced this model in 1977. The key argument advanced by him is that in the situation of uncertainty the policy implementers manipulate, maneuver, cajole or use authority legitimate or otherwise, to implement policy. This process reflects and give impression that politics is being played as a game to maximize their influence and power base. The policy implementation takes a back stage hence implementation looks like, a game for self promotion. It becomes a game of power politics on the pretext of implementation. Bardach's also indicated that implementation is a political process. This is partially correct but it is not that simple. There are so many factors and situations which emerge during implementation which have to be dealt on their merit whether politically or bureaucratically. Having said all that this implementation has relevance but not much work has been done on this approach and not enough research has been carried out. Hence this approach remains at the periphery of implementation.

The real culprit of policy failure is an administrative system which in most of the cases is outdated, inflexible and opportunistic for those who administer it. Policies need to be directly linked to the plans, programmes and projects so as to make policy implementation deliberate set of activities by putting a policy into effect. The government is the key stakeholder to implement the Public Policy because it has been entrusted to achieve goals and objectives within stipulated timeframe and allocated resources articulated in authorized policy statements. The interest in the implementation of Public Policy and measuring the results among the public, media, elected officials and even students of public policy is of insignificant degree. The key reason for this lack of or declining interest is the complexity and nitty-gritty of administrative machinery and government bureaucracy responsible to implement the policy. For politicians, implementation is the responsibility of executive which is prime facia correct, but the support at the higher echelon has to come from elected representatives especially for the allocation of resources and availability of funds.

The non-elected persons had not gone to the travail of being elected hence they do not get into the tedious details of administrative agencies. Also the rules of business of the administrative machinery may not permit them to intervene at this level. The public in general and private interests in particular do take interest in policy implementation but remain at the periphery for different reasons. Hence the implementation of policy remains the most neglected area of public policy cycle.

Time and again a question is raised about the definition of implementation. The variation of definition, particularly in social sciences is a common feature. However a working definition of implementation can be suggested. The implementation is an organized activity by government which is directed towards the achievement of goals and objectives articulated in authorized policy statement. The definition would have been mentioned in the introduction of this chapter but it was deliberately avoided so that the readers do not get into the semantics and lose concentration of actual implementation issues.

The policy designers usually do not give serious attention to implementation and how the goals will be achieved in the real-world setting. It has been observed while reviewing some policy documents in the sectors of education, health, environment, youth (For Pakistan) and was observed that none of policy documents contained proper or implementable Action Plan. However, one page in a 100 pages policy report may be allocated to the policy implementation and that too is superficial. The casual and non-professional attention to policy formulation and the disregard for implementation is a key reason for policy failure. The policy implementation prospects look dismal both in developed and developing countries because of the high expectation of people and conservative bureaucracy. However the policy implementation can be accelerated and qualitatively improved if some of the major pitfalls are avoided. The necessary steps for effective policy implementation are as follow.

Implementation has three stages, "First...a series of logical steps – a progression from interaction through decision to action – and clearly see implementation starting where policy stops. Secondly...distinguish two definite steps in formulating interactions: Policymaking – their initial conditions – and creation of programs which form the inputs to their implementation process. Thirdly, implementation as a process of putting policy into effect, a process which is mainly concerned with coordinating and managing the various elements required to achieve the desired ends"[8].

The minimum requirements for policy implementation include   a) Personnel   and   financial   resources b) Administrative and technical capacity of implementers and c) Political (legislative & government of the day) Executive (Bureaucratic & Administrative) and Judicial (Judicial department / ministry) support.

Figure - 4

Policy Implementation

Conceptual Clarity	Administrative Structure
Operational Goals	Support of Policy Constituency
Leadership	Change Management
Conflict Ideologies	Monitoring and Evaluation

i.   *Conceptual Clarity*

Policy needs to be conceptually sound, clear and simple to understand and stated in terms of desired changes to be achieved during the life of policy. It has been often observed that policy documents has lofty and un-achieving objectives and mention everything possible in that sector. This is not the proper way to develop or formulate policy.

At this step implementation agencies should be clearly defined, timelines must be established and respected. It is important that policy should mention cost estimates for each objective to be achieved. There is a note of caution that policy should neither be loaded with very long list of objectives nor with heavy terminology and difficult words. Policy is not a theory rather a manifestation of people's aspiration for the benefit of public at large especially in the social sector.

ii. Administrative Structure

It is imminent that effectively working administrative structure must be in place with properly qualified and trained staff. The delegation of responsibility to the existing agency, organization or department needs to be assigned. If a new arrangement has to be made than the new organization has to be created through proper legislation with necessary administrative and financial authority.

One extremely important element in the implementation is that it needs to be understood by all stakeholders that policy implementation is done at local levels. It often happens that policy makers are far away and quite unaware about the implementation of the program which emanates from the policy. Similarly the Organization/ Department responsible for program implementation is unaware that a particular program is being implemented as an outcome or one of the objectives of public policy. There is a serious dilemma of social distance between policy makers and those implementing programs. Hence the lesson is that the policy stipulations and programs must be well understood by the personnel responsible for implementing the program.

iii. Operational goals

The policy goals are long term objectives which can be measured generally after the policy implementation is completed. This does not happen in most of the cases because the policy implementation is not a static exercise and continues to be modified based on the observations of program monitoring. It also happens that change in command of the government priorities. Hence it is absolutely necessary that operational goals which can also be called program activities must be defined in the form of deliverables. These must be clearly identified with timelines, resources allocation and availability and implementation mechanism which means who will do what, when and how? By the same token each program activity undertaken in the policy implementation would yield measurable results. The operational goals can also be referred as deliverables a term used often in policy and program documents. The programme activities are monitored internally and frequently whereas the program objectives are measured through the evaluation process. The evaluation is usually done at the completion of the program but there is no bar or constraint to undertake program evaluation any time during the implementation process. However in this evaluation which is called the process evaluation, the evaluators need to mention the limitation of this exercise in terms of time, resources, support mechanism, technical assistance etc.

iv. Support of Policy Constituency

Public Policy is framed and then left to several ministries, department, and organizations for implementation. Each of these institutions chalk-out different programs emanating from policy. What happens during this process is that government somehow loose the vigour and will to support the policy. At this stage the advisory groups, legislative oversight and interest groups can play important role. If the policy does not have a strong support for implementation it usually remain in a lurch. Education development in Pakistan is one of the most neglected sectors because it has no constituency. Allocation of resources to sector of education and training is only nominal. It is less than 2% of GDP for education which leads to stunted growth of an inefficient system. The result is the quality and access to education at all levels Primary, Secondary, Higher remains dismal. A quick survey of small village or some rural area would immediately reveal that education is a very low priority. Their need and demand is job, food, water, roads, health and then education. As a consequence it is important that policy which needs to be implemented to achieve operational goals must have a dynamic constituency. The defense policy gets a large portion of financial allocation, defense programs are well implemented and operational goals are achieved because it has a very strong, powerful, and dynamic constituency i.e. Armed Forces.

v. Leadership

The meaningful policy implementation demands that leadership at different tiers of management structure is a necessary element. In this context leadership is not limited only at the top level but it is more important at the local level where the policy needs to be implemented. The middle tier of the leadership chain also plays a key role between the top levels to the local level. In a poor policy implementation show down reveals that all the three levels i.e. top, middle and local are equally important depending on the assigned task. Aristotle, a Greek sage and philosopher, suggested four major qualities of a leader.

a) ***Justice:*** It means that leader must adopt a fair policy, demonstrate objectivity, honesty and impartiality. The element of integrity, righteousness and even-handedness in dealing with colleagues and co-workers is necessary.

b) ***Temperance:*** Leader at all levels of policy implementation demonstrate self restraint, self control, avoid excess and be moderate. The moderation in behavior and working keep a good balance and leads to control among co-workers.

c) ***Prudence:*** Modesty, caution and carefulness are necessary qualities for a leader to adopt and cultivate. Leader needs to be careful to avoid undesirable consequences and use the discretion judiciously specially in allocation of responsibility and authority.

d) ***Fortitude:*** Courage in pain and adversity are necessary basis for properly implementing policy. There would be situation which breeds frustration such as the financial resource constraint, missing date lines, workers behavior and the fear of failure. It demands resilience, stamina, determination and guts to face challenges whether coming frequently or occasionally.

In certain situations, leadership qualities demand humor and wittiness. Morality, ethics and probity need to be practiced as personal examples.

vi. Changed Management

Management is not a static function, It has to be dynamic which changes and modifies in different circumstances and situation. Perseverance and resilience with necessary flexibility are necessary skills for changed management. Since policy is prepared in long term perspective and its implementation usually takes longer than expected. Hence it is imminent, but not sufficient condition, that necessary technical and budgetary means should be timely provided. Even more important is that the capacity of its personnel (or Human Resources) needs to be upgraded or modified according to changed situations and realities.

Neither the management is static nor the ground realities, hence, do the management of implementation remain on the vigil for policy implementation. If the implementers do not modify the leadership style as per the dictums of changed management then the policy implementation would be done through remote control. This means one person or a small group of people sitting for away would like to control or remote control the implementation at local level. This method has not worked to implement policies and achieve laid down objectives.

vii. Conflicting Ideologies

In policy implementation two rules are generally followed. First is the *Laissez-Faire*, which means ipso-facto, keeps the government hands off. Second, employ the principle of subsidiary, which means in simple terms let the local level control and implement policy whenever feasible. The people at local level desire that government authority and control should be minimal in implementation process. They are inherently doubtful of government and bureaucracy. The people at high pedestal, which controls finances and administrative authority propose public policy solutions to a wide range of social problems and often ignores the nitty-gritty of the possibility of implementation. As a result well intentioned policies and programs have failed primarily because of implementation done in the situations of uncertainty and poor methodology. In the subsequent chapters some policy analysis in different sectors would be presented which are Pakistan specific. Further clarity would emerge from the policy analysis. A well known American economist, Milton Friedman made the following remarks before the Joint Economic Committee of Congress, about the implementation of public policy.

i)   When in doubt, stay out

ii)   If something must be done, understand the behavioral dynamics and change the rules of the game without spending money.

iii)   If you must go further, finance activities but do not administer an agency. That is, hire a private contractor and do not try to produce the goods or services directly through government. (Sastee Roti Scheme failed in Punjab because Government was implementing and controlling the program). Instead find a private firm or contractor to do this job.

iv)   When government must finance something make sure that the money goes directly to the beneficiaries, not through indirect channels.

v)   If government must finance and administrator, competition must be permitted as a yard stick to gauge success and cost.

vi)   When government must obtain resources it should purchase them in the markets.

vii)   When government produces good or service, it should, when possible charge the users a pro-rated cost, not give away the good or service.

viii)   Only as a last resort when all the above has failed, should government finance, administer and deliver the good or service free of charge.[9]

viii. *Monitoring and Evaluation*

One of the most neglected fields in policy cycle is monitoring and evaluation. Why it is important? The monitoring and evaluation is meant to measure results and if it is not done you cannot tell success from failure. If you cannot see success you cannot reward it. If you cannot reward success you are probably rewarding failure. If you cannot see success you cannot learn from it. If you cannot recognize failure, you cannot correct it. Finally if you demonstrate results which means policy implementation is successful.[10]

References

[1] A comprehensive and meaningful analysis is available in a book "Good Governance and Result Based Monitoring" by Dr. Sarfraz Khawaja, Islamabad: 2011

[2] Allama Iqbal Open University: p63

[3] Derthick, Martha. New Towns in Town, Washington, Urban Institute, 1972

[4] Pressman, J. Waldavsky, A. Implementation: Berkeley: University of California: 1973

[5] McMaster, J.C. 1979. Implementation Analysis: An overview: In new developments in public sector management: Concept papers and reports. Canberra: Australian National University: p144

[6] Lipsky, M: Street-level Bureaucracy: Dilemma of the Individuals in Public Service, New York, Russell Sage 1980

[7] Bardach E. The Implementation game: Cambridge MIT, 1977

[8] Sapru, R.K: Public Policy: Art and Craft of Policy Analysis: New Dehli: PHI Learning: 2010: p222

[9] Wayne Hayes, Ph.D: 5/26/2009: http://Profwork.org/pp/study/define.html

[10] Khawaja, Sarfraz: Good Governance and Result Based Monitoring: Poorab Academy, Islamabad: 2011: p141-142

5

POLICY ANALYSIS
Is it a gateway to Policy Science?

"Policy analysis is one activity for which there can be no fixed program, for policy analysis is synonymous with creativity, which may be stimulated by theory and sharpened by practice, which can be learned but not taught"[1].

The dynamics of public policy analysis has been viewed and understood by social scientist in different ways. Political scientist interpret policy analysis overwhelming from the government realm as they are keen to relate this how government functions at different levels and how much and in what ways public policies affect the market and private life. Small number of policy analyst does not appreciate or deliberately avoid understanding the influence of political context on the development and implementation of public policy[2].

Sociologists view as how and when the public policy analysis would influence social institutions and social behavior. The political sociology explores the link between

society and government. The major concern and
contribution of sociologist in the analysis of public policy
is to devise and develop evaluation methodologies, measure
the effectiveness and impact of public policies and
programs. Policies also develop a relationship with people.
This relationship remains very diverse depending upon the
status and influence of the group[3].

Economists understand public policy analysis from the
market perspective. They focus more on resource allocation,
money matters and cash flows to different ministries and
departments and how it effect market dynamics and private
life. The collection of tax revenue, distribution of resources,
monetary and fiscal policies, and the quality of expenditure,
allocation-wise or unlawful determines the efficiency and
equitability of policy analysis[4].

The identification of broad cultural and contextual
factors has been the key factors to influence public policy
analysis. This view has been expressed by historians.
People from diverse backgrounds have given extended
attention to family and health policy[5].

What is Policy Analysis?

The purpose of policy analysis is to measure the
efficiency and effectiveness in the context of achieving
policy objectives. These objectives could be political,
economic or social and how the policy implementation has
made the optimal use of available resources within the
existing constraints of a given system. "This is necessary to
measure the cost of different policy options in view of the

expected benefits. Analysis is a step by step approach to assess the design, implementation (process) and outcomes of public policy. It requires the quantitative techniques as well as qualitative methods and the conclusion would be drawn while juxtaposing different categories of analysis. By any standards of measurement, policy analysis is a complex exercise which has to be done by the professionals who have knowledge and experience of this work. Policy analysis is done in varied situation by different people with diverse background and sophisticated research skills. Professionally done analysis would be helpful in modifying policies, improving implementation process and sharpen the outcome.

Policy analysis requires the use of basic social sciences research methodologies, however for more technical aspects of quantitative analysis, other techniques such as multiple regression, cost benefit analysis, trend analysis, sensitivity analysis are used. The case study method is now considered a useful tool also.

Sometime a question is raised that which policies need to be analyzed? As a principal all policies required analysis but the common practice is that the formal written policies, legislated and emanated from government ministries, departments and institutions get the priority for analysis.

This mostly applies to social policies such as population welfare, transportation, social welfare, women, health etc. However some policies are not analyzed professionally because of the iron curtain which has been placed around them. These include nuclear policy, defence policy, science policy etc. There are other policies which are considered semi sacred and get a protective treatment for analysis which include fiscal policy covering taxing, spending and deficit levels and monetary policy which include money supply and interest rates. Despite the protection the outcome of these policies on the health of economy and its impact on people make them the target of public wrath based on the performance.

However the economic policies are analyzed professionally and critically by the lending agencies, i.e. The World Bank, Asian Development Bank, IMF, and donors – bilateral and multi-lateral. It is observed even these analysis are sometimes biased to protect the interest of lending organization. There is a note of caution in any kind of policy analysis that analysis should never be impressionist but it would be systematic. Also the policy analysis done by the government officers and officials are usually not objective hence it should be done by professionals not employed by government.

Objectives

Every policy has certain goals to achieve within stipulated time and specific resources. How we know that a policy has achieved its objectives or otherwise? The key reason for policy analysis is to determine about the extent of success a policy has achieved in obtaining the goals. There are general methods to analyze policy both in qualitative and quantitative terms which include case studies, survey research, statistical analysis and comparative policy model analysis. The use of evaluation criteria by using the (CIPP model) Context, Input, Processes and Product would be useful vehicle for policy analysis. Similarly another comparable way for analysis is Input, Process and Output (IPO Model). Both these (CIPP & IPO) models are useful for evaluation studies and often used for policy analysis for best policy performance measurement.

The policy analysis by any method is not a prescriptive behavior rather it is an analytical exercise. It is necessary to have a research / evaluation design for policy analysis but there is no road map. The map would emerge as one moves along on the road in an organized way with clearly defined targets. The road map milestone would be set as one moves on the road as to which direction you want to go. In other words if the focus of policy analysis is limited to finances then you have to choose the methods accordingly and if it is divulging more on in-depth qualitative behavior then case study approach would be useful. For a more comprehensive output of policy analysis, a combination of different techniques and methods would be useful. The area of interest and the purpose of analysis determine what type of methods would be used to conduct analysis. As an example how would one go to analyze social welfare policy? Although it could be both the number of people benefiting but more important would be the quality of life which need to be improved through the social welfare policy. Hence what is needed is to focus on those indicators which measures the quality of life and that would be access to health services, availability of doctor/paramedical staff, availability of medicine, emergency treatment, and proper immunization facilities especially for children. Those indicators are important in the context of the quality of Health Services. The access to clear water, basic education facilities, adult learning, etc. are also included. Hence the qualitative aspects are important for the analysis and measurement of social welfare policies.

Approaches to policy analysis

There are generally three approaches available for policy analysis and all are influenced by terminologies used by the economics. The first one is micro-level analysis and its primary aim is to focus and identify the most effective and efficient means to achieve policy goals at grass roots. It would be done through the monitoring and evaluation of different projects which emanates from policy provisions. This would identify whether the projects have achieved qualitative objectives? The efficiency is usually measured in the context of the financial resources and effectiveness is measured on the basis of output or deliverables.

The second approach extends its scope to meso scale and its interpretation generally emanates from political nature. This approach is also known as process approach and tries to explain what process and means are adopted and also explains the role and influence of stakeholders. This resembles to a bottom up approach of policy analysis because of the participation of larger number of people, interest groups, professionals and all those who are directly or indirectly, positively or negatively affected by the policy stipulation and implementation. It is also assumed that process approach would be useful instrument to identify different options for the mitigation of problems.

The third approach to analysis is the meta-policy approach and its scope has been extended to macro-scale and its interpretation focus on structural reforms. The factors may be political, economic, cultural, social and administrative which would be identified through this analysis. This requires structural changes in the existing institutions. One key element which has received greater attention in the present time is the issue of good governance. This term has been used frequently but commonly misunderstood. It is not limited to the policies and outcomes of the government rather the importance it entails. Its characteristics are Accountability, Participation, Predictability and Transparency. Brief description of each variable is given below.

Accountability (Building Government Capacity)

"The accountability of public institutions is facilitated by evaluation of their economic and financial performance. Economic accountability relates to the effectiveness of policy formulation and implementation, and efficiency in resource use. Financial accountability covers accounting systems for expenditure control, and internal and external audits"[6]. This requires establishing a criterion to measure the performance of public officials and make them answerable for government behavior and the needs of society. This also includes effective policy formulation, implementation and efficient resource utilization[7].

Participation (Participatory Development Process)

"At the grassroots level, participation implies that government structures are flexible enough to offer beneficiaries, and others affected, the opportunity to improve the design and implementation of public programs and projects. This increases "ownership" and enhances results. At a different level, the effectiveness of policies and institutions impinging on the economy as a whole may require the broad support and cooperation of major economic actors concerned to the extent that the interface between public agencies and the private sector is conducive to the latter's participation in the economy, national economic performance (comprising the combined contributions of the public and private sectors) will be enhanced"[8]. People are at the heart of development. They are not only beneficiaries of development but also change agents. This creates an ownership of programmes and policies.

Predictability (Legal Framework)

"Predictability refers to (i) the existence of laws, regulations, and policies to regulate society; and (ii) their fair and consistent application. The importance of predictability cannot be overstated since, without it, the orderly existence of citizens and institutions would be impossible. The rule of law encompasses well defined rights and duties, as well as mechanisms for enforcing them, and settling disputes in an impartial manner. It requires the state and its subsidiary agencies to be as much bound by, and answerable to, the legal system as are private individuals and enterprises" [9] . It provides for laws, regulations, and policies, which will regulate the society through fair and consistent execution. The rule based system helps ensure that business risks are assessed rationally, transactions costs are lowered and government arbitrariness be minimized.

Transparency (Information Openness)

"Transparency in government decision making and public policy implementation reduces uncertainty and can help inhibit corruption among public officials. To this end, rules and procedures that are simple, straightforward, and easy to apply are preferable to those that provide discretionary powers to government officials or that are susceptible to different interpretations. However, well intentioned the latter type of rule might be in theory; its purpose can be vitiated in practice through error or otherwise"[10]. It enables access of information to general public, clarity about government rules, regulations and decisions, this would mean reducing uncertainty about government decisions and public policy implementation, and also inhibit corruption among public officials.

Politics of policy analysis

Policy analysis is a political activity hence it is sensitive for ruling elite. Politicians or political party in

power is often in a position to influence the methodology
and outcome of analysis. The relative success and
usefulness of public policies has to be determined
empirically as well as within the context of societal norms.
Having said that, it would be quite difficult to suggest
precision in the methodology of policy analysis. As the
disciplinary boundaries are overlapping – some time
separating but at other merging – as the discipline of public
policy has borne out from political science. This bifurcation
makes it difficult to suggest a precise definition of policy
analysis. However its merit is that, it poses more challenges
to specialists, academicians and practitioners to devise a
common understanding of policy analysis. Another aspect
or difficulty in policy analysis is the changing nature of
policy objective by the present government or the next one.
It means that policy analysis is a dynamic activity and not a
static exercise. It oscillates, at the time of formulation,
between aspirations and reality and that theme persists
during the implementation and analysis.

The operative part of policy analysis covers. "Three
main areas of modern life: (1) the government, (2) the
economy, and (3) private life. Each of these institutions is
complicated, multilayered, and dynamic. Government
expands and contracts, what transpires in the market
changes over time. And the boundaries of private life are in
constant flux. Because the boundaries overlap, some
aspects of life fall into more than one arena. Which aspects
of life fall under the institutional reach of government, the
marketplace, or private life are constantly shifting? Policies

can structure the relationships within and among each arena"[11].

The trichotomy of public policy among government, economy and private life prima facie looks complex hence it is intricate in practice as well. As a case in point could be an education policy. The government formulates education policy for primary education. The policy is supposed to provide opportunities of access and quality for all segments of society but more so, for disadvantaged sections of society which may include poor people both in rural and urban areas and females. Then follows the implementation which also is the responsibility of the government.

The next question is about the relationship of economy with the government. Every component of primary education policy require certain inputs – i.e. School building, Furniture, reading material (text books), teacher's appointment and salaries, supervisory staff and an evaluation system. All these are one part but the other part comes from parents who decide to send their children to school. The question of accessibility to school – financial, geographical, cultural, and social – is very important for parents. The poor family may not afford to send a child to school because of unaffordable financial expenses on notebooks, stationery and textbooks etc. It is also closely related to opportunity cost for the family. A child working on the agriculture land, household worker, helper, etc. earns some money every day – certainly a meager amount by any standard. Now the parents have to balance and make decision to send a child to school and spend money from their pocket or send a child to work so that he/she can earn some money for the family for food security. The economy plays an important role in decision making for the family.

The third part in the trichotomy is private life. A child not going to school can take care of younger siblings, help mother in household chores, go to the field to assist father and above all no cash would be spent by the family which is already living below the poverty line. The private life is immensely affected by the public policy for primary education. What is the lesson in the context of public policy and analysis? The key issue is to restructure the relationship within and among each arena of government economy and private life. In other words state (government) has to ensure accessibility to education for poor families, financial system (economic) has to provide basic expenses for education and parents (private life) need to understand the long term return and benefits of education. This could be in the form of improved job opportunity, chances of upward mobility, disciplined and organized family, healthy environment and responsible citizenry.

Since the policy analysis requires skills and focus of multi-dimensional nature evolved from diverse disciplinary basis hence policy analysis has no epistemology or methodology exclusive for this purpose. It also means that any number of methods can be used for policy analysis which may constitute broadly quantitative, qualitative or the combination of both these approaches. Some of the 'policy analysis methods' have been mentioned in this chapter for the benefit of comprehension as well as for operational use. The comparative policy analysis would compare more policies with each other to understand the implications of a variety of different policy changes. Some time as a result of policy analysis certain policy outcomes emerge quiet dominantly but not intended in the policy design, implementation and inputs.

Figure - 5

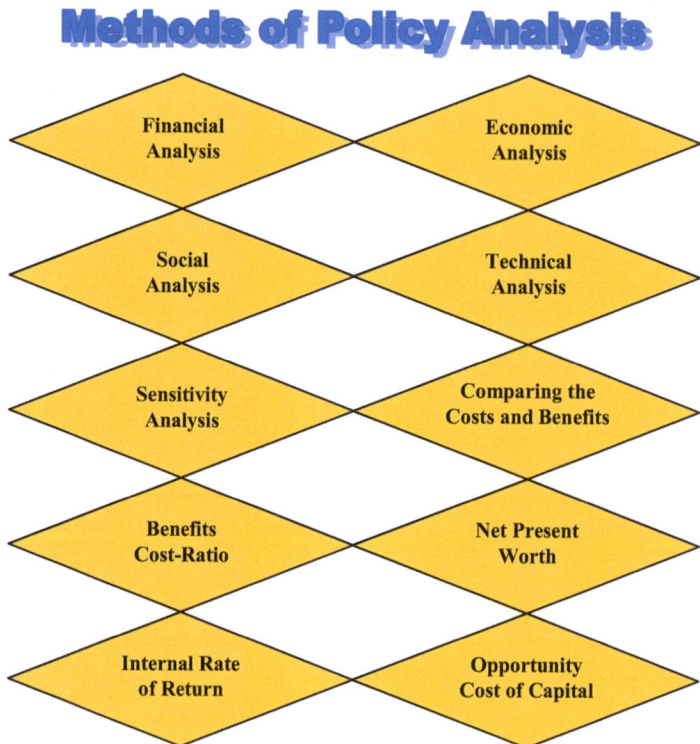

Methods of Policy Analysis

Financial Analysis

Economic Analysis

Social Analysis

Technical Analysis

Sensitivity Analysis

Comparing the Costs and Benefits

Benefits Cost-Ratio

Net Present Worth

Internal Rate of Return

Opportunity Cost of Capital

Financial Analysis

The financial aspects of policy preparation and analysis are concerned with the financial impact on the policy and on each of its various components. It invariably answers questions such as what investment funds will be needed and when? What will be the operating expenses when the policy implementation is underway? Whether these expenses depend on budget allocations or other sources would produce sufficient revenues to cover its investment? It calculates the financial viability of investment at market prices from the point of view of different sectors of economy which are vigorously competing for financial resources.

Economic Analysis

The economic aspects of policy analysis deal with determining whether the implementation would likely to contribute significantly to the development of the total economy and whether its contribution will be large enough to justify the investment of scarce resources on it. This analysis takes into account the point of view of the society as a whole. In economic analysis, firstly, taxes, duties and subsidies are treated as transfer payments. Secondly, some market prices are also changed to reflect better "accounting prices". Thirdly, in this analysis, interest on capital is never separated and deducted from the gross return since it is a part of the total return to the capital available to the society as a whole, and it is that total return, including interest, which this analysis is designed to estimate for the society as a whole.

The techniques of economic analysis help to identify policy components that make the greatest contribution to national income. The economic analysis basically allows for remuneration to labour and other inputs either at market prices or shadow prices which are intended to be approximately true opportunity costs. Implicit objective of economic analysis is the maximization of growth of the economy.

Social Analysis

It has now become conventional to treat efficiency pricing as the subject of economic analysis in contrast to social analysis, which requires extending the analytical framework to incorporate distributional judgments. Such judgments are essentially of two kinds: firstly, Is consumption optimally distributed between contemporaries (intra-temporal) and secondly, Is it optimally distributed between generations (inter-temporal)?

For the purposes of analyzing policy from social point of view, distribution weights are calculated and applied to the steam of cost and benefit calculated at efficiency prices (shadow prices). The objectives underlying the social analysis are the distributional impact i.e. equity.

Technical Analysis

The analysis for determining the technical impact, including the choice of appropriate technology, for the development is made by the technical section (e.g. the location, supply of raw-materials, process to be used, market demand, infrastructure, supply of managerial, technical and other types of manpower, building size, design, scope for future expansion of the plant, the building and capacity etc.) as well as the earlier experience of carrying out previous policies in the same sector. The knowledge and experience of other countries of executing similar methods can also be helpful. The technical tests and yardsticks to be used for technical analysis differ from one country to another in different sectors.

The technical data and information and cost effectiveness of an energy policy will differ from the specifications and technical details of Transportation Policy.

The specifications of machinery and equipment, the category-wise performance of managerial, technical manpower and their specified skills will also be scrutinized. As such, each policy component has to be tested and scrutinized on its own merits keeping in view all its related technical details, costs and objectives in the context of rapidly changing nature and style of technology.

In cases, where high-level technology is involved and the country has little or no experience in that particular line, foreign consultants are also employed to prepare specific jobs. The technical experts of the Planning and Development Ministry / Departments can be trained to apply almost similar procedures / tests.

Sensitivity Analysis

This analysis studies the impact that changes in cost and benefits would have on the profitability or present value of project which emanates from public policy. As an example a 10% increase in construction cost might reduce the internal rate of return from 15% to 9% for project A, but only from 15% to 12% for project B. As such, at the time of appraisal of projects it is necessary that sensitivity analysis be carried out to see whether it would be beneficial if there is time and cost over-runs. It should be specially seen whether the benefits are likely to have the same escalation in value as the cost. Further, it is necessary to know whether the projects could still be beneficial despite changes in the cost structure.

Comparing the Costs and Benefits

Whether one is calculating a financial, economic or social profitability, a key part of the analysis will be to work out the actual flows of income and expenditure of different programs. The basic principle of the "Cash-flow" as the term suggests, is that income (inflow) and expenditure (outflow) should be carried out at the time they actually occur. Hence concepts, such as, that of "depreciation" and "sinking funds" are not required.

Policy analysis involves the comparison of programs taking several years, which have differently shaped future costs and benefits streams and also comparison among alternative programs of different sizes. The usual method of addressing these problems is through discounting. There are three discounted measures of project worth: Benefit-Cost Ratio (BCR); Net Present worth (NPW); and Internal Rate of Return (IRR). These are described as under:

Benefits Cost-Ratio (BCR)

Both the benefit and cost streams are discounted at a rate considered to be closer to the opportunity cost of capital and the ratio between the present worth of benefits divided by present worth of the costs is determined. When the ratio is equal to one or above, the program is treated as viable.

Net Present Worth (NPW)

The most straightforward discounted cash flow measure of project worth is the Net Present Worth, often abbreviated as NPW. The Net Present Worth is calculated by subtracting present worth of costs from present worth of benefits discounted at opportunity cost of capital. When the Net Present Worth is positive, the project is said to be desirable. (A project with positive NPW at 12% opportunity cost of capital is considered justified for implementation).

Internal Rate of Return (IRR)

It is the discount rate, which just makes the NPW of the cash-flow equal to zero. This discount rate is termed as the internal rate of return and is the weighted average earning power of the resources used during life of a project. The cash flow is discounted to determine its present worth. By trial and error, one discount rate is found which is too low and which leaves a positive present worth, another discount rate is found which is too high and which leaves a negative present worth of the cash-flow stream. The formal selection criterion for the IRR measure of Project Worth is to accept all projects having an IRR equal to or greater than the opportunity cost of capital.

Opportunity Cost of Capital

All the three measures of project worth must be related to the opportunity cost of capital. For private enterprise, the opportunity cost of capital will be a weighted average of the borrowing rate for funds and an acceptable price-earnings ratio for equity shares.

The opportunity cost of capital is the return on the last (i.e. marginal) investment, which could be made where all the available capital is fully invested in the most remunerative alternative manner.

The formal selection criterion for the BCR and NPW is to accept all the projects, which have BCR equal to or greater than unity and NPW, positive, when discounted at opportunity cost of capital.

The analysis is carried out by the Appraisal Experts before launching the implementation of a policy and evaluated either during the implementation or at the completion of the program or both of the Planning and Development Departments, Project Appraisal Section and the experts of the sponsoring agencies themselves.

Qualitative Methods

Outcome Studies

The policy analysis measures the policy effectiveness in terms of bringing positive changes in the lives of people; what impact policy has made in improving the social conditions of society or a particular group of people; whether the level of poverty or the people living below the poverty line has decreased; how much the rule of law has been observed or is being practiced; has any policy improved the level of punctuality in the government offices;

how far the crime rate particularly the snatching or theft of automobiles and cell phones have decreased or increased and so on. All these policy outcomes are not tide up with the financial cost at present but this does not mean that these outcomes do not incur expenditure. In this case the cost element has been deliberately set aside so that the outcome of policy is seen more objectively and not over shadowed by the component of cost. However this should be understood that money remains an important input for policy implementation.

Different categories of researches can be designed and undertaken to measure the outcome of policies which can be termed as outcome studies. The nature of study design could be illuminative, qualitative, experimental, quasi-experimental or others. As an example poverty could be measured through different methods with reference to the poverty reduction policy; Do health policies in Pakistan for the last years have improved the health status of the disadvantaged section of the population particularly poor people, rural inhabitants, females, children and others?

Without getting into the quagmire of statistics, Pakistan does not have a primary health care system strong enough to manage expanded programme of immunization for children against communicable diseases. It is not only the weak system but considerable segment of society in rural areas which are mostly illiterate, are not convinced about the efficacy of polio and measles vaccines. This disbelief and the poor policy implementation outfit would be the result of a bad or poorly planned policy. The prevention and treatment of malaria, tuberculosis, typhoid and flu need to be improved. During 2012 the province of Punjab, with the population of about 85 million, was struck with the dengue fever, a virus infested with the bite of mosquito. It created tremendous amount of fear and few hundred deaths but the policy was prepared and implemented with such an earnest and commitment that during the month of July 2013 no causalities have been reported. The policy was multi pronged based on awareness, advocacy, cleanliness, mosquito killing oils, service delivery, immediate blood test, establishment of special units in the hospitals, separate duty roaster for doctors treating the ailment etc. The policy outcome abundantly reflected the usefulness and successful implementation of this component of health policy. Another example could be mentioned with reference to Millennium Development Goals. There is no doubt in anybody's mind that these goals would not be achieved for Pakistan by 2015. There has been too much of buzz from the donor agencies about the MDGs. The Table No.7 demonstrate that the targets are too far from Pakistan's reach.

Table – 7: Analysis Of Expected Delay In The Achievement of MDGS

	1990	2009	Average Annual Achievement	2015 Target	Gap between 2009 – 2015	Expected Achievement Year	Expected Delay in Years
Under-5 mortality rate (per1,000 live births)	140	95	2.3	47	38	2030	15
Infant mortality rate (per 1,000 live births)	120	74	2.4	40	28	2027	12
Proportion of fully immunized children 12-23 months (%)	25%	60%	1.8%	90%	30%	2031	16
Maternal mortality ratio (per 1,000,00 live births)	550	300	13	140	160	2027	12
Births attended by skilled birth attendant (%)	-	30%	3%	90%	60%	2035	20
Contraceptive prevalence	12%	30%	1%	90%	60%	2075	30

The 'donors', as they would like to be known as "partners in development" are many including major UN agencies i.e. UNDP, UNICEF, UNESCO, FAO, etc, bilateral and multilateral donors and to cap it all there is The World Bank and The Asian Development Bank. The WB and ADB are lending agencies like development banks. One thing must be put into proper perspective that all these agencies/organizations are neither 'donors' nor 'partners in development'. They are essentially and by practice the bureaucratic organizations pushing their agendas or the desire of their masters especially in developing countries and making useless interventions in the entire development process. In fact these agencies are obstacles to right kind of development as they impose their own misplaced, ulterior motivated project oriented and financially unsound development on the citizens and cities of this country[12]. Some of these are so 'good' & 'competent' to sell electric blankets in Somalia during the summer months.[13] In such an environment the achievement of MDG's is not only elusive but misguided. However this does not absolve Pakistan to fulfill its responsibilities as a signatory to MDG's and put its house in order where corruption is rampant, governance is dismal, rule of law is diminishing fast, power shortage is crossing limits (electricity load shedding is now 18 hours in 24 hours) and crime is surging like an organized activity.

Case Studies

The case study as an instrument of analysis or methodology for teaching in social sciences emanates during the mid 20th century. Before that the case study as a method of inquiring and follow-up was used in medical sciences. The history of a patient, step by step covering all possible influences, habits and surroundings would develop into a comprehensive and in-depth knowledge base about the causes of disease or diseases and the effects of medicines taken during the time span of sickness. This case study method further gained currency when the Harvard Business School was started and faculty realized that there were no textbooks available for graduate program in business administration. The first major step in this

direction was taken to interview leading business
practitioners and write detailed accounts of what these
managers have been doing in terms of policy formulation to
establish business, sales promotion, human resource
development, corporate relationship and other important
elements of business management. As a result the best case
studies in the discipline of business administration have
been developed by Harvard University faculty and most of
these are available in the archives. These cases have been
developed keeping in view with particular learning
objectives but are thoroughly discussed in the classrooms
and modified or improved before publication. "Case studies
are analyses of persons, events, decisions, periods, projects,
policies, institutions or other systems that are studied
holistically by one or more methods. The case that is the
subject of the inquiry will be an instance of a class of
phenomena that provides an analytical frame – an object –
with which the study is conducted and which the case
illuminates and explicates."[14]

The case study as an instrument of policy analysis
involves the systematic and comprehensive description
which includes policy formulation, implementation,
monitoring and evaluation.[15] Here the 'poverty reduction
strategy paper' prepared by government of Pakistan could
be termed as official policy. This intended policy was a
combination of confused policy interventions. The
emphasis was laid upon high economic growth which has
been a positive part but the distributional aspect of
economic and social opportunities and benefits to the

weaker and deprived strata of population remained in a lurch. The massive corruption and bad governance neither improved the economic growth rate nor the distribution aspect. As a result the larger number of people joined the already staggering number of persons living below the poverty line.

There are different types of case studies. The categorization is useful to simplify the definition of case studies which includes Descriptive; involves starting with a descriptive theory. The subjects are thus observed and the information gathered is compared to the pre-existing theory, Intrinsic; type of case study in which the researcher has a personal interest in the case, Explanatory; case study that is sometime used a prelude to further, more in depth research. This allows researchers to gather more information before developing their research questions and hypotheses, Exploratory; this type of case study primarily intended to do causal investigation which can be used as a starting point or kick start the process collectively; this involves the study of inputs and behavior pattern of a group of individuals and what collective contribution has been made and then Instrumental; which occurs when the individual or group allows researchers to understand more than what is initially obvious to observers. [16] This also indicates the unintended outcome of policy.

The case study method for policy analysis is a useful tool but with some limitations. The major one is that the validity of one case study cannot be generalized for many or all cases of similar nature. The major reason has been that assumptions, inputs, surroundings and above all the behavior of an individual or group of individuals are varied to unknown extent. However the case study method remains an important qualitative and occasionally quantitative tool. The following case study demonstrates as how this method could be helpful for policy analysis.

Sense and Sanitation by Sheela Patel[17]

Bombay is the financial capital of India with some of the highest property values in the world. Half of its ten million people pay incredible prices for homes. The other half live in informal settlements; more than a million of them on pavements in makeshift structures of bamboo, plastic, cloth, wood and tin. These people pay a high price too, though the currency they had over is not rupees but their own health, living as they often do without water or sanitation of any kind.

Yet the Bombay Municipal Corporation (BMC) is ambivalent: 'We can't give toilets to slum dweller; this will encourage people to migrate to the city!' they say, or: 'The slums along the highway should have sanitation so foreign visitors don't have to see this embarrassing sight of squatting people with umbrellas along the road.' As if people were flocking to Bombay to enjoy the luxury of public toilet blocks, or the psychological comfort of tourists should be the primary motivation of municipal sanitation programmes!

Or else they say: 'Don't the poor deserve the same as everyone else – an individual toilet?' or: 'Since poor communities don't maintain public toilets, let's give them toilets in their own home so they will be forced to keep things clean.'

Everyone, it seems, has an opinion about how to solve the problem of sanitation in informal settlements. But what do the residents who live there, the people on the footpaths and in the slums, believe is a workable solution?

In 1984, I and 12 other people formed the Society for the Promotion of Area Resource Centres (SPARC). We sought to create an organization which would make space for poor communities to focus on issues which concern them, to understand why they face certain problems and then to reflect on the solutions. Over the last ten years, through our alliance with Mahila Milan – a national network of women's collectives – and the National Slum Dwellers Federation (NSDF), we have used this approach to address many issues, including land tenure, shelter, employment and credit.

The way women living on pavements in the Byculla area of Bombay formulated their opinion on toilets illustrates our approach. We visited slums both with and without public toilets, and the few government-constructed tenement blocks in which each dwelling has an individual toilet. Through these site visits and numerous discussions the women arrived at an assessment of the status quo.

Less than half of Bombay is linked to sewers. In most slums the residents either defecate in the open or – in the few locations where they exist – use community latrines. Municipal maintenance is infrequent and poor, and the number of users per toilet is far too high. The toilets are dirty, uncared-for, overflowing and often unusable.

In slums without toilets people created makeshift arrangements which emphasized privacy, but not the disposal of faeces. In slums with toilets the number of users could be as high as 500 people per seat. Little children never got a chance to use the facilities when adult men were line up waiting. In the government-constructed, multi-storey tenements, women were very unhappy to have an individual toilet inside their homes. In all the areas visited women had taken the drastic step of blocking it up. Many slums have low water pressure; toilets begin the stink, and since the tenement is only one room a dirty toilet next to the cooking area presents a serious health hazard. 'If we have to cope with a dirty toilet,' the women said, 'it is better that it is outside the house – we have other uses for that space'.

Having completed the rounds of other informal settlements, SPARC, Mahila Milan and NSDF began to develop their own views. They agreed a preference for community toilets with a ratio of one toilet for every 25 people – a block of four to five seats could be shared by 20-25 households who would jointly manage them. The blocks would include separate seats for men and women, an outside open channel over which the children could squat and a flushing mechanism which would draw their waste into the main collection pit.

When we enter into dialogue with the authorities this is now the basic formula we present to them as the people's solution. It is not perfect. It is not ideal. And it is not permanent. But it represents a pragmatic solution which will make basic sanitation available to all the poor people in the city and establish a partnership between city authorities and communities.

The collective, hard-earned experience of SPARC, Mahila Milan and NSDF suggests that proactive dialogue must be properly prepared for by the participants. Each group must make a substantial investment so that it can come to the negotiating table with a clear sense of what is important to them and what is not, what contribution they can make towards the solution and what concessions would be acceptable.

In 1989-90 we surveyed slums in ten cities. We helped local city federations identify a core team of community leaders (men and women) who visited all their informal settlements. Almost invariably sanitation was identified as one of the most persistent and serious problems they faced. For example, in Kanpur, a city in the State of Uttar Pradesh in the north of India, the slum dwellers surveyed their area and found they needed 500 toilets. They suggested that municipal officials study their proposal and, if it were acceptable, construct a number of toilet blocks which the communities would then maintain.

We began training slum dwellers in other cities to organize them and to enter into dialogue with the municipal administrations. We also ensured that federations were able to visit each other's settlements to gain ideas and confidence. These types of support provided both capacity-building experience and tangible evidence – assets which helped their participation in the city's decision-making process.

We are now participating in a project in Bombay which will provide 20,000 toilet seats for one million people living in the city's slums. According to our data collection there are at present just 3,000 toilet seats for these people; 80 per cent of the toilets are not fully operational and need to be torn down or repaired. Negotiations to explore how communities can be assisted to take on construction, maintenance and management of toilets are in progress.

We and the communities with which we work have come a long way in the ten years since women pavement dwellers first began to discuss the problem of toilets in their ideal settlement. As more and more communities, women and city officials co-operate they become more capable of refining the solution, adding new dimensions and adapting to different contexts. This improves the material condition of people living in informal urban settlements. But, more importantly, it is a process of empowerment and involvement. Once people start talking about toilets other things follow.

Meta analysis

The common problem which emerges here is the definition of Meta Analysis or in simple words, what is meta analysis? The term, as some of us may perceive is considered modern but its use dates back to 12th century in China. A famous philosopher, Chu His built up his philosophical theory by summarizing a series of related literature which he called a 'Theory of systematic Rule'. Again during the 17th century Meta analysis was used in the studies of Astronomy. In the early 20th century the collated data from several studies of typhoid inoculation was seen as the first time the Meta analysis approach was used to aggregate the outcomes of multiple clinical studies. In this backdrop this technique has been used quantitatively as well as qualitatively for policy analysis. The term meta analysis was coined by Gene V. glass and he stated "my major interest currently is in what we have come to call.....the meta analysis of research. The term is a bit grand, but it is precise and apt.....Meta analysis refers to the analysis of analyses"[18]

In precise terms Meta analysis is the Analyses of many studies / researches done on the same topic. The methodology, sample, time frame and universe may vary and so would be the results. If the studies, including in the meta analysis, have been done by adopting faulty methods, unreliable data and poor design hence the quality of meta analysis would be wrong and inconsistence.

It means that a good meta analysis of badly designed studies would result in bad / wrong findings. Having said that, there are certain advantages of Meta analysis. This may include that the results of Meta analysis can be generalized to a larger population subject to the condition that the research studies have adopted proper research methodology. The Meta analyses also lead to the precision and accuracy of estimates can be improved as more data is used. This also increases the possibility to detect problems of data. If the inconsistency is found in sampling error then the corrective measures can be adopted to address the issue of quantified analysis. Another advantage of the Meta Analyses is that it explains variation between studies in terms of outputs and outcomes.

References

[1] Aaron Wildavsky, Speaking Truth to power? New York: John Wiley, 1979: p3

[2] Gummer, G. (1990) The politics of Social administration: Managing organizational politics in social sciences: Englewood Cliffs, N.J: prentice Hall.

[3] Rossi, P. & Freeman, H. (1993). Evaluation: A system approach. Newbury Park. CA: Sage publications.

[4] Garfinkel, I. (Ed). (1982). Income-tested transfer programs: The case for and against. San Diego: Academic press.

[5] Minow, M. (1990). Making all the difference: inclusion exclusion and American law. Ithaca, NY: Cornell University press.

[6] Asian Development Bank, Governance Sound Development Management. Manila: ADB: 1995: p8.

[7] Khawaja, Sarfraz: Combating Corruption through Good Governance and International Cooperation in Pakistan: 2002-2007: India: Machillan Publishers: 2009 pp160-161.

[8] Asian Development Bank, Governance Sound Development Management – Opcit: 1995: p9.

[9] Ibid

[10] Ibid

[11] Einbinder, Susan D: Policy Analysis.

[12] Sherbano, Afiya: The development buzz: The NEWS International: Islamabad: November 28, 2006. p6.

[13] A comprehensive account about the International aid agencies is given in 'The lords of Poverty: The power, prestige, corruption of the International Aid Business' by Graham Hancock published by Macmillan limited, London in 1989.

[14] G. Thomas (2011) A typology for case study in social science following a review of definition discourse and structure. Qualitative inquiry 17, 6, 511 – 521.

[15] Mognihan, D.P (1970) Maximum feasible misunderstanding: New York. Free press.

[16] Cherry, Kendra: About.com guide.

[17] Sheela Patel is one of the founders and the current director of SPARC. Write to P.O.Box 9389, Bombay 400026, India for more information. This case study has been taken from the course of studies prepared for public policy of Allama Iqbal Open University – Islamabad. (Bibliography No.2)

[18] Glass G.V (1976) Educational Researcher 5 (10): 3-8.doi:10.3102/0013189x005010003.

6

ANALYSIS OF
MADRASSA EDUCATION

How perception and reality are at variance?

Introduction*

M adrassa (The Arabic word for school) as an
institution of formal learning has been in practice for
several centuries. During the first twelve centuries of
Islamic history the institutions of Madrassa and Jamia
(University) were not confined to religious education alone.
However most of Madrassas were located in the mosques
and as such the mosque became a citadel for educational,
social and religious activities. After the fall of Baghdad in
the 13th century, the distortions began to appear in the
Madrassas but in the latter part of the 18th century
Madrassa system shrank into a limited religious learning.
This situation aggravated further in the middle of the 19th
century in the Indian Sub-Continent. During the last one

---

* The evaluation of Madrasah Reform Project was done in 2007, when the
another of this book was working as Monitoring and Evaluation Specialist with
the Planning Commission on Contract. The evaluation design, conduct of
research and preparation of draft report was prepared by the author under the
guidance of Gen. (R) Mohammad Zubair, Member, Implementation and
Monitoring , Planning Commission, Planning and Development Division,
Government of Pakistan: Islamabad.

hundred and fifty years, Muslim thinkers made efforts to reform the Madrassa system by complementing religious education with secular education, introducing new emerging disciplines and facilitate the mobility from Madrassa system of education to the Formal Education System and vice-versa.

Madrassa Education: International Perspective

In Philippines during the 9th century the Islamic religion started spreading in some parts of the country through business community which traveled to Middle East for trade. The major breakthrough in this regard was the establishment of Muslim Association of the Philippines in 1920 which started making efforts to protect the rights of Muslims in the country. But in 1950 a regular Madrassa system of education was introduced in the Philippines. By 1955 it was properly accepted and recognized by the Government but without any major interference in that system.[1]

Indonesia, the biggest Muslim country in terms of population, had started the Madrassa system of education in the early 19th century mostly in rural areas. This system was brought to the country by the Indonesian pilgrims. After performing Haj they became motivated to introduce the value system which they observed in Makah and Medina. These Madrassas were well supported by the villagers and financially Madrassa were self sustaining. Their base remained in the rural areas with focus on conservative value system which were in vogue in the society at that time. This system continued for about a century but the changes started to appear in the early decades of the 20th century when the large number of Hajjis started supporting the Madrassa system of Education. These Hajjis were more influenced by the scholars of Al Azhar University of Egypt. The number of Madrassas started increasing mostly in urban areas and in 1912 "Mohammadia Tehrik" started with a focus on "Reformation" in Madrassas. In 1930 large number of Madrassas started establishing in Indonesia but no cleavage developed between the "Conservatives" and "Reformationist". One key commonality between the two schools of thoughts was that the medium of Instruction in both the systems was Arabic language. Hence the graduates of Madrassa system were fluent and well versed in Arabic language. As a result they had lot of interaction, exchange programs and training facilities with the Al Azhar University. In Turkey most of the Madrassas have Arabic language as a medium of instructions and Al Azhar also has a significant influence on these Madrassas.

One of the youngest Muslim countries in the World, Bangala Desh, has an amazingly successful system of Madrassa education. The number of National Madrassas is 6500 where Dars-i-Nizami is exclusively taught. The number of teachers is these Madaris is 13000 and the total enrollment of students is 1462500. These are private Madrassas and do not get any money or grant from the government. These are known as National Madrassas and English language is a compulsory subject but it is not the medium of Instruction. The second category of Madrassas in Bangala Desh is called *Higher Madrassas*. The number of these Madrassas is 6906 and number of teachers is 11720 and the total enrollment of students is 1878300. The Government of Bengal Desh provides 80% of salaries to the teachers and 75% of the Research and Development also come from the government kitty. The examinations of these Madrassas are conducted by the Madrassa Education Board. These Madrassas teach Dars-i-Nizami as well as modern subjects and disciplines.[2]

There are four commonalities in Madrassa system of education in these countries, except Pakistan. I) there is no conflict between the formal and Madrassa system of education. ii) The policies of respective governments do not interfere with Madrassa education. iii) There is no indication that the governments of these countries want to control or dominate the Madrassa education. iv) None of these countries have the record to pass any ordinances or stipulate harsh laws for these Madrassas. There are some lessons for Pakistan to learn from these experiences.

But the sectarian divide within the Islamic religion did not allow Madrassas to flourish side by side with modern/secular education. However significant expansion and changes happened in Madrassa system in Pakistan after its independence in 1947. The main reason for growth in Madrassas was the failure of public education system (government) to respond to the needs of society and unable to provide access to education to the low income group. The schools did not keep pace with the growing population and economy. The quality of education was low and at best mediocre.

Madrassa Registration in Pakistan[3]

Prior to 1970 every Madrassa in the Pakistan was registered with the government under the Societies Registration Act of 1860. This undertaking accorded recognition to Madrassa in the same manner as opening of a school in the private sector. But the lynch pin of Madrassa system of education was the Mohtamim (Head Teacher) with exclusive control to award certificates to the passing students. The name of Madrassa has little significance in this regard. The identification of curriculum, selection of text books and the mode of examination remained the sole discretion of the Mohtamim. The Wafaq/Boards did exist but their role was limited to liaison between and among Madrassas and Government. During the late 1970s and early 1980s the graduates of Madrassa pressurized the government to give due recognition to their certificates/degrees and provide equivalence as FA, BA, MA etc of the formal system. As the circumstances were favorable in the early 1980s the Madrassa graduates approached the Higher Education Commission (at that time University Grant Commission) and with the blessings of government the Madrassa degrees/certificates got the equivalence with formal system of education. This gave impetus to the growing number of Madrassas. The Afghan war against Russia and massive support of USA to Jihadi Tanzeem were enabling factors for Madrassas to flourish.

The schemes of studies which cover the syllabus of Madrassas are spread over sixteen years. This period is divided into six grades. The following table reflects the grades of Madrassa education and its equivalence with formal education system as well.

Table – 8: Grades of Education in Madrassas and Formal Education[4]

Grade	Level	Equivalence with Mainstream System	Class	Duration
Ibtidai	Nazra (Primary)	Primary	1-5	5 years
Mutawassit	Hifz (Middle)	Middle	6-8	3 years
Sania Aama	Tajvidh, Qirat, (Secondary)	Matriculation	9-10	2 years
Sania Khasa	Tehtani (Higher Secondary)	Intermediate	11-12	2 years
Aalia	Moquf-Alaih (College)	Bachelors	13-14	2 years
Alamia	Dora-e-Hadith (University)	Masters	15-16	2 years

Madrassa Reform Project

The Government of Pakistan launched Madrassa Reforms project (2003-2007) with the estimated cost of Rs.5759.395 million. The major objectives of the project were to mainstream Madrassa education system with formal education, open lines of communication with Ulmas who run Madrassas, teach formal subjects in 8000 Madrassas, offer financial incentives and provide teaching learning materials / equipment. It was expected to educate about 1.5 million students (both male and female) and employ to 32000 teachers in Madrassas. The evaluation exercise undertaken in 2007 found that about 468

Madrassas benefited from the project instead of 8000 (5.8%), 2291 teachers were appointed against the target of 32000 (7%), 50,000 students benefited from the teaching of formal subjects against the target of 1.5 million (3%) and Expenditure was 2.8% of total allocation of Rs.5759.3 Million. The Ministry of Education submitted a summary to the Prime Minister in April 2007 who decided that: "Planning Commission should undertake an Independent evaluation of the current project in consultation with other stakeholders and recommend if a revised project would be appropriate.

Schism Starts

As per previous practice Madrassas were registered with the government and affiliated with the respective Wafaq. During 1993-94 the government stopped the registration of Madrassas. The rationale was to discourage and if possible stop the establishment of new Madrassas. The government did not realize that by stopping the registration, neither the demand for Madrassas nor the number of Madrassa decreased but a confrontation started between the government and Madrassas.

The Madrassa registration again opened in 1995 by the government but the schism has been widened and the dye has been cast. This murky and half baked policy was in vogue when the events of 9/11, 2001 took place. The distrust between the government and Madrassas further increased when the government asked all the Madrassas to re-register under the Madrassa ordinance of 2001. In due course of time the Societies Registration Act of 1860 was amended with Societies Registration Ordinance of 2005, which provided that

i) The Deeni Madaris existing before the commencement of the Societies Registration (Second Amendment) ordinance 2005, if not already registered, shall get themselves registered under this Act upto the 31st December, 2005;

ii) The Deeni Madaris which are established after the commencement of the Societies Registration (second Amendment) Ordinance, 2005, shall get themselves registered within one year of their establishment.

iii) Every Deeni Madrassa shall submit annual report of its educational activities to the Registrar.

iv) Every Deeni Madrassa shall cause to be carried out audit of its accounts by an Auditor and submit a copy of its audit report to the Registrar.

v) No Deeni Madrassa shall teach or publish any literature which promotes militancy or spreads sectarianism or religious hatred.

This time the registration form required that each Madrassa must provide the financial details of the Madrassa. The Madrassas were reluctant to provide the financial information. The Wafaq / Madrassas argued that no private formal educational institution provides financial details to the government then why to target Madrassas alone. The lack of trust between Madrassas and the government increased with every passing day.

Government on its part decided to launch a Madrassa Reforms Project (MRP) to mainstream Madrassa education with formal education and minimize the schism. But the leadership of Madrassas – that is respective Wafaq, did not support MRP because of the lack of the trust on the government with regard to the registration issue.

Wafaq-al-Madaris

There are five Wafaq-al-Madaris working in Pakistan. Each Madrassa is affiliated with one of the Wafaq as per the *Maslak* of the Madrassa. Each Wafaq is responsible to prepare curriculum and scheme of studies, prescribe text books, hold examinations and issue certificates to the students of Madrassas of their respective *Maslaks*. Brief information of Five Wafaqs is given below:

i.   **Wafaq-al-Madaris al-Salafiah**: This Wafaq represents Sunni and Ahl-e-Hadith institution. This was established in 1955 at Faisalabad.

ii. **Wafaq-al-Madaris al-Arabia**: This Wafaq constitutes of Sunni, Hanafi and Deobandi institutions. It was established in 1959, and is located in Multan.

iii. **Wafaq-al-Madaris al-Shia'a**: This Wafaq of Shia'a institution was established in 1959, at Lahore.

iv. **Tanzim-al-Madaris**: This Wafaq represents Sunni, Hanafi and Barelvi institutions. It was established in 1960 at Lahore.

v.   **Rabitah-al-Madaris al-Islamiya**: This is a non-sectarian Wafaq and it recognizes all schools of

Islamic thought/jurisprudence. It was established in 1983 and located in Mansoorah, Lahore.

It is interesting to note that all the Wafaq have their Headquarters in Punjab. Four of the Wafaq were established in late 1950s and only one was established in 1983. The role of Wafaq-al-Madaris would be critical in any future reforms in Madrassa education system hence it is important that all the five Wafaq should be major stakeholders in the new project.

Affiliation of Madrassas with different Wafaq in 2000 is shown in this table.

Table – 9: Number of Madrassas Affiliated with various Boards, 1988-2000[5]

Organization	1988	2000
Wafaq-al-Madaris al-Arabia (Hanafi, Deoband)	1840	1947
Tanzim-al-Madaris (Hanafi, Barelvi)	717	1363
Wafaq-al-Madaris al-Salafia (Ahl-e-Hadith)	161	310
Wafaq-al-Madaris al-Shia'a	47	297
Rabitah-ul-Madaris al-Islamiya (Mansoora)	-	191
Others (not affiliated)	96	2653
Total	2861	6761

The five Wafaq agreed to constitute one representative body with the name of *Ithad-i-Tanzeemat-Madrasia-Denia* (ITMD) to negotiate with government on different issues on behalf of all Wafaqs. In 2001 a memorandum of understanding was reached between ITMD and the Ministry of Religious Affairs (representing federal government) that a modified ordinance, with the concurrence of ITMD, would be issued by the government. Subsequently this ordinance would become an Act of Parliament (both federal and provincial) as agreed between ITMD and the governments. This has not yet materialized. It created a cause of further misunderstanding between the government and Madrassas.

The Madrassa Reforms Project suffered the credibility gap between the government and ITMD (Also Wafaq and Madrassas did not trust the government). The problems were further compounded when the international factors and foreign funding came into play for Madrassa Reforms. The ITMD, Wafaq and Madrassas perceived that the government has become pro-west at the cost of the ideological identity of Pakistan, faces problem of legitimacy, its war on terror, enlightened moderation and too much interference with Madrassas have all been cited as the reason for credibility gap.

In regard to the MRP, another observation/reaction from the Madrassa lobby is that Pakistan is the second largest participant in the Cambridge System (A and O level) of examination of England, (first being the England herself) hence contributing maximum fees in foreign exchange to England but the government has never looked at the A and O level course of studies, curricula or text book. Some of this may be against our National Interests.

Working of Wafaq-ul-Madaris

i) Each Wafaq has an independent setup. The Wafaq is headed by a president (sadar), who has overall responsibility of the Wafaq but his position is mostly ceremonial. At operational level, the Secretary General of the Wafaq is responsible to administer and manage the affairs of Wafaq. The Majlis-i-Amal is the apex body, constituted through the election by the members of Wafaq Madrassas. The operational body of the Wafaq is Majlis-i-Shoora elected from the Majlis-i-Amal by its members. All the decisions of Majlis-i-Shoora are ratified by the Majlis-i-Amal, a bigger body.

ii) Each Wafaq prepares curricula for the respective *Maslak* of different grades/levels.

iii) Each Wafaq is an examining body as well as certificate/degree awarding authority. This can be compared with Board of Intermediate & Secondary Education as examining body but the board does not prepare curriculum.

iv) Each Wafaq is also a policy making as well as a representative body for the respective Maslak and authorized to negotiate with the government on behalf of the Maslak.

v) Each Madrassa must be affiliated with one of the Wafaq because non affiliated Madrassa has no identity, no examining body, no set of curriculum, no authority of issuing certificates/degrees; as such the affiliation becomes an issue of survival for the Madrassas.

vi) The Jamia Hifsa & Jamia Fareedia were de-affiliated by their Wafaq because the Wafaq did not approve of their approach for the implementation of

Islamic rule. However, neither Jamia Hifsa nor
Fareedia violated the code of Wafaq i.e. following the
curriculum and presenting students for examination to
Wafaq. But with the cancellation of affiliation, these
two Madrassas would have faced problems of
equivalence of their degrees.

Employability of Madrassa Graduates

The argument advanced by the Madrassas and their
Wafaq with regard to the employability of graduates is that
most of modern subjects i.e. English, Mathematics, physics,
computer science are already included in the curricula of
studies in the Madrassas and these subjects are taught by
properly qualified teachers. Hence their employability is as
good as the graduates of formal system. The employment
avenues are as follows:

i)   The number of Madrassas is rising constantly and
rapidly. This also means the increased enrollment of
Madrassas. One interesting feature is that the Madrassa
enrollment is not exclusively confined to poor, orphans
or destitutes but is also increasing with the students
coming form rich business families, wards of
bureaucrats and senior military officers. The expanding
number of Madrassas and their students need more
teachers which Madrassas system of education
provides.

ii)   The number of Mosques is increasing with the
increasing population. Another reason for rapidly
increasing the number of Mosques is the reaction of

Muslims in general and Pakistani Muslims in particular about the unjust and sometime barbaric policies of the west. The Imam Masjids are required for each mosque hence graduates of Madrassas provide the service.

iii) As the certificates/degrees of Madrassa are equal to regular/formal system of education, hence they are getting employment as teachers in formal school system at primary, middle and secondary level. The argument is also advanced that the quality of Madrassa teachers is as good as the quality of teachers trained in the formal system. Some of the Madrassa graduates have even obtained PhD degrees hence they are not behind in the race of education and employability.

iv) There were 378 M. Phil and 240 PhDs teaching in Deeni Madrassas[6].

v)   The Madrassa graduates are also self employed by starting small business especially in rural or semi urban areas. They are doing quite well in this profession.

vi) Some of the Madrassa graduates who are well versed in English got well paid employment outside Pakistan.

vii) Another argument is that the employability of Madrassa graduates is as good or as bad as the graduates of the formal university system of Education. The unemployment is rampant of the graduates of formal education system.

Modernization of Madrassa Education in Pakistan

This Madrassa Reforms Project (MRP) also got impetus because of the stipulation of Education Policy of 1998-2010. Which narrates to integrate Deeni Madaris with formal education system, some formal school subjects like English, Mathematics, General Science, Economics and Pakistan Studies shall be included in the curricula of Deeni Madaris and their Asnads at Matric, Intermediate and Graduate levels shall be equated with the formal education. All the willing Madaris shall be provided suitable financial assistance for payment of salaries to the teachers.[7] The same policy recommended the establishment of Deeni Madaris Board for uniform standards of Deeni Madrassa Education through registration, standardization of curricula and examination system, equivalence of asnad, award of foreign scholarships, grant in aid and financial assistance by the government, a Deeni Madrassa Board shall be established.[8]

It is important to note here that the number of Madrassas and their enrollment keeps on fluctuating. The following table shows this paradox.

Table – 10: Number of Madrassas and Enrollment

Name of the Organization	Year	No. of Madrassas	Enrollment
Ministry of Education[9]	1980s	8424	1312262
Institute of Policy Studies[10]	2002	6761	1065277
Ministry of Education and Statistics Division[11]	2006	11491	1518298
Ministry of Religious Affairs[12]	2007	17000	2000000

It is difficult to determine the exact number of Madrassas in the country but one conclusion can be drawn from the above table that there was a metriotic increase in the Madrassas after 2002. The increase was 39.7% in four years from 2003 to 2007 with an average annual increase of 9.9%.

Objectives

The Madrassa Reform Project (MRP) was approved for a period of five years by the government of Pakistan on 7th January 2004 with an estimated cost of Rs.5759.395 million. The major objectives of the project were as follows.

- Mainstream Madrassa education system with formal education.
- Open lines of communication with Ulmas who run Madrassas to impart formal education in addition to religious education.
- Teach formal subject in 8000 Madrassas to bridge the gulf between Madrassa education and formal education.
- Provide financial incentives (one time grant to each Madrassa).
- Provide teaching learning materials, computers, printers and sports kits.

Expected Results

It was envisaged that the project after completion would yield following results.

- Project will establish and strengthen lines of communication amongst the Madrassas and Government.

- Educate about 1.5 million students (both male and female) of eight thousand Madrassas to be included in the Madrassa Reforms Project to teach them formal subjects from primary to intermediate level to enable them to continue their studies in colleges and universities.

- Provide opportunity of employment to 32000 teachers for teaching formal subjects at different level in Madrassas.

- Provide incentives through books, furniture, computers, printers and sports facilities to improve education system of Madrassas.

Status of Project Implementation

The completion date of the Project was 30th June 2007. Based on the office record, monitoring reports observations and evaluation it was found that

- Against the target of 8000 Madrassas, only 468 included in the project during four years (5.8%).

- Expenditure level was only 2.8% (Rs. 161.2 million out of Rs. 5759.3 million) of the allocated amount.

- 32000 qualified teachers were to be appointed in Madrassas but only 2291 teachers could be posted (7%).

- Province of Baluchistan did not establish Project Management Unit.
- Project Madrassas in Punjab were administered and managed by the Federal Project Implementation Unit (FPIU), Ministry of Education, Islamabad. Hence Punjab did not participate in the Project.
- National Steering Committee --- the apex decision making body never met.

Implementation Agencies

The key implementation agencies at Federal, Provincial and area levels were

- Ministry of Education.
- Provincial Education Departments.
- Education Departments of AJK/FATA/FANA.

Terms of Reference for Evaluation

The Planning commission prepared the terms of reference for the Evaluation:

- Despite allocation of sufficient funds by the Government, the implementation has been extremely low. Analyze the impediments in the implementation.

- Has the project been able to bring desired changes in Madrassas, which was to 'bridge the gap (mainstreaming) between religious education and formal education system? Identify the reasons that hindered mainstreaming the Madrassa reforms.

- Were the funds provided to different Madrassas used on the agreed components of the project and if not, what were the reasons?

- Why the provinces showed lack of interest and shied away from the project? What reasons could be identified for this reluctance?

- How far the Ministries of Religious Affairs and Interior complemented their efforts with the Ministry of Education for implementation of project.

- Based on the findings of Evaluation what interventions/strategies would be included in the new project?

Evaluation Model: (CIPP)

The CIPP model of evaluation has been used and adopted for the conceptual frame work for evaluation of Madrassa Reforms Project. The description of the Model is as follows:

C = Context, I = Input, P = Process and P = Product.

Context

- Describe the boundaries of the Project to be evaluated.

- Define its relevant environment.

- Delineate the actual and the desired conditions.

- Identify unmet needs and unused opportunities.

- Diagnose and analyze problems.

- Monitor the system to maintain a current baseline of information and, provide a basis for widespread communication and control

- Look for new emerging value orientation.

Input

Provide information for determining how to use resources to achieve project objectives by assessing the following:

- Relevant capabilities of the responsible agency.

- Strategies for achieving goals.

- Design to implement selected strategy.

- Information on whether outside assistance is required.

- Objective should be stated operationally.

- Operational plan should be employed to implement the strategy.

Process

Provide feedback for the following variables:

- Detect or predict defects in the procedural design or in its implementation.

- Provide information for programmed decision.

- Maintain a record of the procedure as it occurs.

- Identify and monitor potential sources of failure in a project.

- Decisions about the implementation of the project to be made by project managers.

- Notify the features of the project design and describe what is actually taking place.

- Continuous feedback about the project.

- Information is delineated, obtained, and reported as often as required – daily, if necessary especially, during the early stages of project.

Product

Its purpose is to measure achievements not only at the end of the project but as often as necessary during the project implementation. The methods are:

- Devising operational definition of objectives.

- Mastering criteria associated with the objectives of the activity.

- Comparing these with predetermined, absolute or relative standards.

- Making rational interpretation of the outcomes using recoded context, input and process information.

Sample Selection

The ten percent selection of sample Madrassas was done on random basis with the help of provincial governments. However, efforts were made to cover as many districts as possible and all schools of thoughts (Maslak) were to be represented in the samples of Madrassas.

Table – 11: Sample Madrassas for Evaluation

Province / Area	Project Madrassas	Sample Required	District Covered
Islamabad Capital Territory	11	02	01
Sindh	46	06	06
Khyber Pakhtoon Kha	81	09	09
Balochistan	53	09	07
Federally administrated Tribal areas	92	09	-
Federally administrated Northern areas	51	08	-
Azad Jammu Kashmir	78	10	04
FPIU (Punjab)	56	13	13
Total	**468**	**66**	**40**

Evaluation Design

The design of the evaluation which included the review and the analysis of the projects documents from 2003 to 2006, preparation of the terms of reference, development of questionnaire and tasks for the evaluation team were drafted.

Micro Testing of Questionnaire

The questionnaire prepared for the evaluation was micro tested on August 25, 2007 in two Madrassas of Islamabad. The rural female Madrassa was Jamia Fatima-tul-Zuhra located at Bhera-pull, Bhara Kahu Islamabad. The other Madrassa was for male students in urban area named Jamia Naeemia located at G-9/3, Islamabad. The data collection officers for this micro testing included two officers from the evaluation section of the projects wing of Planning Commission (including a female officer) and two officers from Federal Project Implementation Unit, Ministry of Education Islamabad. These officers were provided orientation about the questionnaire, briefed about the interview techniques and how to record responses. The questionnaire was revised and modified on the basis of micro testing and observation of data collection officers. The final questionnaire is placed at the end of this chapter.

Training of Data Collection Officers

The team of twenty data collection officers was nominated. One day orientation/training (September 22, 2007) was provided to these officers about the interview techniques, questionnaire and how to record responses etc.

Data Collection

These data collection officers visited the Madrassas in Punjab, Sindh, KPK, Balochistan, and Islamabad from September 23 to October 2, 2007. Each province/area coordinated the visit of these officers to the respective Madrassas. The data collection officers did not face any problem during this process and gave back the filled in questionnaire for evaluation on October 3, 2007. The data from FATA, FANA and AJK was collected by the representatives of the respective Governments.

Data Compilation

The data compilation and analysis process started on October 3, 2007 and completed on Oct 6, 2007. Several reports were generated for this analysis and used for the preparation of this report.

Presentation of Data and Findings

In the Madrassa Reforms Project 468 Madrassas were provided project inputs. These included trained teachers, teaching learning resources, computer & printers, introduction of new subjects, financial assistance and sports kits. More than 10% Madrassas sample was taken for evaluation which covered 40 districts all over Pakistan. A questionnaire with 59 items was used for this exercise.

Table – 12: Status of Madrassa Buildings

Category	Percentage
Pakka Buildings	90.91%
Kacha Buildings	7.27%
No Buildings	1.82%

Madrassa system of education has almost the same percentage of pakka buildings as that of government school of formal system. But 7% of government schools are without building whereas less than 2% of Madrassas are without buildings. Hence financial resources for construction of Madrassa building would be a minimum requirement.

Table – 13: Available Physical Facilities in Project Madrassas

Category	Percentage
One Class Room	25.45%
Two or more class Rooms	74.55%
Computer Lab	60.00%
Library	90.91%
Staff Rooms	84.27%
Cafeteria	52.73%
Toilets	90.91%

The basic physical facilities required in an educational institution are mostly available in the Madrassas. It is important to note that there are 41% government schools which are without toilets/latrines but in Madrassas around 92% have toilet facilities. The availability of library and staff room facilities for government primary schools in rural areas is very low but it is 92% and 87% respectively in Madrassas.

Table – 14: Number of Students in Project Madrassas by Income Level

Category		Percentage
Poor:	Monthly earning of Rs. 3000 per month or less	75.39%
Lower Middle:	Monthly earning of Rs. 10,000 per month or more	20.81%
Upper Middle:	Monthly earning of Rs. 20,000 per month or more	3.59%
Well to do:	Monthly earning of Rs. 50,000 per month or more	0.21%

The common perception that only poor and destitute student are enrolled in Madrassas is not entirely correct. However the majority of students are from poor families. But the children of middle class families are also joining the Madrassas. The percentage of well to do or rich families is still insignificant as Madrassa student.

Table – 15: Teachers Availability

Category	Percentage
Full Time	90.06%
Part Time	9.94%

The issue of teacher absenteeism has usually plagued the formal system of education. But strangely the teacher availability in Madrassas is very high. One possible reason could be the commitment of teachers of Madrassa to remain available to the students for teaching

Table – 16: Academic Qualifications of Teachers

Category	Total %	Male %	Female %
Below Matric	14.41	63.92	36.08
Matric	21.84	53.74	46.26
Intermediate	19.02	55.47	44.53
Bachelor	21.55	55.86	44.14
Masters	22.73	84.31	15.69
Any Other	0.45	33.33	66.67

There is high percentage, more than 80%, of teachers who have academic qualification of matriculation or higher certification. This is an encouraging sign that these teachers can be trained in PTC, CT, B.ED and M.ED courses in government teacher training institutes.

Table – 17: Professional Qualification of Teachers

Category	Percentage
Hifz	31.05
Dars Nizami	46.24
Any Other	18.30
Untrained	4.41

The professionally qualified teachers are limited to subjects for the teaching of religious education only. These teachers can also be trained in pedagogical skill, subject contents and modern methods of teaching.

Table – 18: Teaching of Primary Level Subjects of formal Education in Project Madrassas

Subject	2003 (%)	2004 (%)	2005 (%)	2006 (%)	2007 (%)
English	34.55	32.73	60.00	54.55	81.82
Mathematics	36.36	34.55	61.82	56.36	81.82
Social/Pakistan Studies	30.91	29.09	56.36	50.91	74.55
General Science	30.91	29.09	54.55	49.09	72.73

There is gradual increase in the teaching of above subjects cited in the table which have been taught in the Madrassa schools at primary level during the project life.

Table – 19: Teaching of Secondary Level Subjects of formal Education in Project Madrassas

Subject	2003 (%)	2004 (%)	2005 (%)	2006 (%)	2007 (%)
English	29.09	27.27	47.27	41.82	47.27
Economics	10.91	10.91	23.64	21.82	21.82
Computer Science	18.18	20.00	34.55	30.91	32.73
Pakistan Studies	25.45	25.45	45.45	41.82	47.27

There is also an increase in the teaching of formal subjects introduced by the project but the percentage of secondary level is less than 50% as against more than 70% at the primary level.

Table – 20: Computers Provided to Project Madrassas

Category	2003 (%)	2004 (%)	2005 (%)	2006 (%)	2007 (%)
Computers	7.27	0.00	10.91	9.09	7.27
Printers	7.27	0.00	7.27	12.73	5.45

The response to the provision of computer to Madrassas looks very low. The reason is that computers & printers were given only to those Madrassas offering higher secondary education. The sample Madrassas which offer education at this level was relatively small and that is the reason for this low count in this table.

Table – 21: Responses of Madrassa Teachers about Project Inputs

(Percentages)

Question	Yes	No	No Response
If new project provides facilities to improve professional qualification (PTC/CT/B.ED would Madrassa teachers' likely to benefit from this opportunity?	98.18	1.82	0.00
Do you think that Madrassa Reform Project enables the students to get employment after completing their education from Madrassa?	49.09	50.91	0.00
Did the Madrassa teachers use computers (where provided), If yes, how many days in a month? Mention below	30.91	61.82	7.27
After introducing new subjects, did you find any change in the general behavior of Madrassa students?			
Students were more playful.	87.27	9.09	3.64
Talking / discussing topics like computers/internet.	63.64	32.73	3.64
Students going outside Madrassa more often.	70.91	25.45	3.64
Did the student participate more in sports activities than before.	78.18	18.18	3.64
Has Computers and Printers provided incentives to improve education system of Madrassas?	32.73	47.27	20.00
Whether Sports goods provided to Madrassas?	58.18	38.18	3.64
Was the enrollment of students of your Madrassa increased because of the project inputs (teachers, teaching learning resources and sports kits)?	65.45	30.91	3.64

Questionnaire for evaluation intended to measure the observations/responses of Madrassa teachers about the project inputs. This table provides the information.

Table – 22: Suggestions for the Next Phase of the Programme

Suggestions	Percentage
Curriculum must include Computer (IT) and English Language Diplomas for Madrassa Students	62.50
Curriculum should be revised (College University)/ Affiliation with Board	35.42
Increase in Pays, funds, of the teachers / supporting staff	31.25
Market Oriented / Vocational Skills should be included in teaching course	20.83
Technical Education like: Software Engineering, Electrician, Mobile Repairing	20.83
Continuation of the MRP Project	20.83
Expansion of Madrassa Building / Provision of hostel	20.83
Books and Sports Kits needed	20.83
Higher Education included M.Ed	12.50

These are the suggestions given by the respondents, in rank order, for the changes required in the next Madrassa Reform Program. The scope of this kind of information can be further extended through Needs Assessment Survey of Madrassas if the next program is to be launched.

Findings

1. The evaluation reveals that there was about 13% increase in the enrolment of Madrassa students every year from 2003 to 2007. The increase in the number of Madrassas during the same period was 8% every year. If this trend continues for another five years the Madrassa enrolment would be expected to reach 3.3 million by 2012. Only 21% of the respondents

(Teachers & Head teachers) agreed to continue the project in its present frame work and inputs. The major changes which have been recommended by the remaining respondents include curriculum revision (62.5%), increase in teacher's salaries (31.2%), availability of books and sports kits (20.8%) and provision of hostel (21%) in the Madrassas.

2. There is no evidence available from Evaluation exercise which suggests that the communication between Madrassa administration and government representatives has improved or even properly established. The Ministry of Religious Affairs used some influence on five Wafaqs for the registration of Madrassas but nothing further happened to properly and effectively implement the project. The Madrassa reforms project provided one vehicle to each Wafaq without defining any role and responsibility to be performed by these Wafaqs in the implementation of the projects. There has also been a significant amount of trust deficit between the government and the five Wafaq which created hurdles in the project implementation. The Wafaq perceived that in the name of reforms, the government was planning to eventually take over the control of Madrassas. However the evaluation found no evidence at all which can suggest that the government has any plan to administer or control Madrassas. As a matter of fact the government is struggling to improve the standards of education and trying to manage the existing government schools efficiently and effectively.

3. A dichotomy was found in the process of implementation of the project. The Madrassas are registered with the provincial Department of Industries because of Societies Registration Ordnance of 2005. The provinces send this registration information to Provincial Department of Aukaf for onward transmission to the Ministry of Religious Affairs. This Ministry supervised and monitor the mechanism and keep record of Madrassa registration at National level. Whereas the Ministry of Education was the implementation agency of the project without having sufficient insight in the working of Madrassas. In addition the Ministry of Education controlled the funds for the project hence in a position to exert more authority. This diarchy has created some tension and misunderstanding between the two ministries at the cost of implementation of Madrassa reforms project. In addition there was a constant tension between the two ministries over the control of turf regarding the project. Each of the two ministries tried to prove the superiority and competence over the other to administer the project. However both were unable to create any viable operational plan to implement the project effectively.

4. The time consuming and long process of Madrassa verification by the Ministry of Interior as a pre-condition to release funds was unnecessary because no such arrangement was required or envisaged in the PC-1 of the Project. It adversely delayed and negatively affected the implementation of the project. The Government of Punjab was reluctant to set up a

Provincial Implementation Unit (PIU) due to its difference with Federal Project Implementation Unit (FPIU) over certain administrative issues. As a result the Madrassas located in the province of Punjab were directly given grants and monitored by the FPIU from Islamabad. Hence the province which has the highest number of Madrassas, about 6000, could not take the imitative forward. The provincial government remained non-serious in the implementation of the project which was manifest from the fact that the federal government provided a grant of Rs: 300 million which was returned to the federal government after two years. The question of ownership loomed large in the provinces and it needs to be addressed seriously for the next project.

5. There has been 13% increase in the enrolment of Madrassas students from 2003 to 2007. This can be attributed to the increased number of Madrassas and rapidly growing population. The information gathered from the evaluation questionnaire, project records, meetings with focal persons and visit to provinces/area headquarters revealed that only 468 Madrassas benefited from the project. The teaching of formal subjects could only be extended to about fifty thousand students against the target of 1.5 million. There is no record that any Madrassa graduate enrolled in any college or university in the formal education sector during the life of the project. The project enabled only to recruit and appoint 2291 teachers against the target

of 32000. Their performance to teach formal subjects was not satisfactory as ascertained from evaluation.

6. It was assumed in the MRP that the provision of certain inputs would achieve the laid down objectives of the project. This has not happened which is evident from the observations made by the evaluators, interview with the policy makers of Education Ministry and provincial education departments. The data obtained from Madrassas does not reflect any change in the Madrassa environment hence any effort of mainstreaming the Madrassa education has not happened. It raises three questions. i) Was the assumption of giving project inputs, without any need assessment faulty? ii) Was the nature of projects inputs inappropriate? iii) Were the assumptions as well as the project inputs inadequate?

7. The project followed supply driven approach (provision of teaching learning resources, sports kits, computers & printers, appointment of new teachers introduction of new subjects and vehicles for Wafaqs. There is no record or evidence that the provision of these inputs were based on any need assessment survey either formally or informally. Hence these inputs had little impact on achieving the project objectives. Was there any impact of computers, printers, stationary items, sets of books and sports kits provided to improve education system of Madrassas? About 21% responded of positive impacts whereas 62.5% recommended the revision of curriculum and inputs.

8. The Madrassa reforms project was complex in scope, inaccessible to certain geographical proximity, sensitive and volatile in certain areas. The overall responsibility of implementation was given to the Ministry of Education which is not an implementing agency by mandate rather an apex body for policy formulation, curriculum development and monitoring. The National Steering Committee, an apex decision making body for the project under the control of Ministry of Education never met during the four years of the life of the project.

9. The time in the release of funds to the Madrassas by the Ministry/ Provincial Department took on average 24 months. This delay causes uncertainty and frustration among the Madrassa administration. The procedure for the release of Grant from FPIU to a Madrassa is as follows:

    i)   Madrassa administration applies for funds and other inputs to FPIU on prescribed Proforma.

    ii) After some scrutiny the FPIU send this duly filled in proforma to the Ministry of Interior. (This procedure is not given in the PC-I, hence the violation of PC-I stipulations).

    iii) Interior Ministry sends this proforma to six different agencies for verification and clearance.

    iv) Each of those six agencies send three different individual, one after the other, for verification of the applied Madrassa for grant. Thus theoretically eighteen personnel of different intelligence agencies visit one Madrassa for verification and clearance.

v) The approximate/'average time is 24 months to complete this procedure of clearance.

vi) Then the FPIU issues a cross cheque (Payees Account) in the name of the Madrassa.

10. The registration of Madrassas at provincial level is done with the Department of Industries. The list of registered Madrassas is sent to the Provincial Aukaf Department. Then the Aukaf Department sends the list to Ministry of Religious Affairs, which after consolidation of list from different provinces sent it to the Prime Minister Secretariat and Presidency.

11. There is no uniform and standardized system of examination and evaluation for the Madrassa students. This creates credibility gap for equivalence and raises questions about quality control.

Recommendations

1. In view of the large increase in the enrolment of Madrassa students (13% every year), who need to be taught subjects of formal education also, it is recommended that Government should take up a Madrassa Reform Program on regular basis instead of a project. The evaluation suggested that 62.5% of the respondents recommended that curriculum should be revised to include computers (IT), diploma in English language, software engineering and mobile repairing.

2. The Ministry of Education has been unable to implement the project and one reason was the diversified nature of stakeholders in the project. The Ministry of Religious affairs did not have the experience and expertise to implement such a big project. For the new Program, two possible options can be considered.

    i)   Out source the project implementation to a private consultancy firm through transparent bidding. The monitoring may be done jointly by the ministries of education, religious affairs and relevant provincial department.

    ii) The implementation at federal level may rest with the Education ministry but the district administration of the devolved local government system would implement the program at distinct level. The Planning Commission would be responsible for monitoring. The implementation agencies at Federal and District levels must be properly trained and tailored in the mechanism of Programme implementation of Madrassas.

3. Madrassa teachers and Mohtamim are the key persons to bring any change in the mindset of Madrassa students. The project has missed an opportunity to transform this change. It is indeed a daunting task but not impossible to achieve. The tone and tenor of Madrassa environment is set by Mohtamim and teachers, hence they are the change agents. The challenge is the preparation of curriculum which has

been suggested by the respondent mentioned in above para. The following information would reveal that how many teachers need to be trained in the next Programme.

Total Number of Madrassa Teachers[13]	55210
Below Matric	23807
Matric	15004
Intermediate	6535
Graduate	4586
M.A	4660
M.Phil	378
Ph.D	240

The major question is how the teachers would fit in the new role of change agents to mainstream Madrassa education with Formal education? It is thus recommended:

i)   That the new Programme must provide professional training to all the teachers holding Matric, Intermediate certificates and BA, MA degrees. This number would be around 30,000. There are more than 150 Teacher Training Institutes (TTI) in the country. On average each TTI would be able to train 50 Madrassa teachers per year. If this methodology is adopted the TTI,s would train all the 30,000 teachers within four years of the life of the new Programme . This would be a critical mass for the change of Madrassa environment.

ii) The teachers identified for training should be provided scholarships to cover 100% expenses

during the training in the Teacher Training
Institutes.

iii) The selection of teachers for training would be
done by the respective Education Departments of
the Provinces / Areas with close collaboration of
Wafaq-ul-Madaris.

iv) The teachers after the completion of training
would get the certificate of Primary Teacher
Certificate (PTC) after matriculation, Certificate
of Teaching (CT) after FA/FSc and Bachelor of
Education (B.Ed) after BA. These trained teachers
would come back to Madrassas with pedagogical
skills, properly trained in subject contents and
possibly the changed mindset.

v) The teachers trained under the Programme would
be qualified to teach in regular Primary, Middle
and Secondary schools. The incentives mentioned
above would enable the Madrassa teacher to join
the training program willingly at the Teachers
Training Institutes. The marketability of their
services would enhance and chances of
employment would increase even if they continue
to teach at Madrassas.

vi) The implementation of the teacher training
program requires meticulous planning and viable
operational plan must be articulated to implement
this component of the Programme. It is
manageable and practical. No new institutions are
to be created. The mechanism needs to be planned
and rigorously executed.

4.   The financial size of the project (Rs.5579.364 million) was too big for the system of project implementation which has limited capacity to absorb these funds. Most of the funds were allocated for the software (teaching-learning resources, recruitment and appointment 32000 teachers scattered all over the country and mostly in difficult to reach areas) and not much hardware (building, equipment, purchase of vehicles). The lack of Infrastructure, non availability of trained manpower, weak financial and accounting systems, cumbersome administrative procedures and lack of ownership by the provinces all led to failure of the project. The next Programme should be planned realistically with clearly laid down implementation strategy.

5.   It is recommended that most of the funds should be allocated for teacher training scholarships for students/ teachers and incentives for good teachers teaching formal subjects in Madrassas. The funds for this purpose should be provided to respective teacher training institute in the tehsil/district. The TTI has the credibility, infrastructure and manpower to disburse funds and above all the reporting mechanism of its activities to the education department of the province. This would enable and reform Madrassa education system to ensure that those who graduate from TTIs would have the opportunity of mobility into the mainstream system of education and on to the gainful employment also.

6. The hiring and appointment of 32000 teachers may
    seem simple with high unemployment rate in the
    country, but it was a complex activity. The teachers
    have to be recruited and appointed all over Pakistan
    specially in the difficult terrain where law and order
    problem further compounded the accessibility to
    FANA, FATA, Baluchistan and NWFP. The
    availability of trained teachers in these areas and the
    reluctance of qualified teachers to teach in Madrassas
    made the task difficult. Thus It is recommended that
    the Teacher Training Institute located in that particular
    tehsil/district headquarter should be given the
    responsibility to identify, recruit and train the teachers
    for Madrassas. This should be done at the time of
    admission of students to teachers training institutions.
    The identified teachers should be provided
    scholarships covering all their expenses during the
    course of training.

7. The appointment of a teacher with one Maslak if
    appointed to a Madrassa with different Maslak has
    created problems. The teacher was not accepted by
    Madrassa administration hence unable to perform
    duties properly and effectively. It is important that the
    Maslak of teacher should be the same as the Maslak of
    the Madrassa. The assistance in this regard should be
    obtained from the Wafaq of the respective Maslak.

8. The five Wafaqs have immense influence and in
    certain ways control the Madrassa education system. In
    the MRP these Wafaqs were provided vehicle one each

to a Wafaq but their role to assist in implementation of the project at best was ambiguous. These Wafaqs are a key player in controlling Madrassas by giving affiliation, recognition of Madrassas; decide about the curriculum and issue certificates. Hence Wafaqul Madaris must be one of key stakeholders to implement the new project along with the respective provincial authorities as identified. The Wafaqul Madaris should be given specific responsibility along with certain accountability of their performance.

9.   The relation between Wafaqul Madaris and the Ministry of Religious Affairs is cordial as compared with the Ministry of Education. It is thus recommended that Wafaq and Ministry of Religious Affairs should share the joint responsibility of: i) monitor the Madrassa Teacher Training Program of Formal education. ii) Qualitative performance of Madrassas. iii) Close and regular liaison with Madrassas.

10.   In the presence of the district administration of the devolved local government system it would have been appropriate to give the responsibility of the implementation of Madrassa reform project to the district level. The committee comprising of District, Tehsil and Union Nazmeens, with district coordinating officers to take the responsibility for the implementation. In FANA and FATA the respective district administration / agencies should have been given this responsibility.

11. The time to release funds to Madrassas can be cut short
to eight weeks instead of two years, if the money is
directly released to Madrassa by FPIU instead of
getting clearance from the Ministry of Interior which
hardly has time and interest in this activity relating to
the project. However this information can be endorsed
to district and provincial governments. The registration
of Madrassa with the Ministry of Religious Affairs is a
sufficient condition for the release of funds to
Madrassas.

12. An autonomous Federal Examination Board for
Madrassas needs to be established under Programme
implementation agency. This Board would only
conduct examinations on the basis of curriculum set by
the Wafaq. If this experiment succeeds, such
Provincial Boards can also be established with certain
changes and modifications. This would enable the
Federal and Provincial governments to know the
enrollment of Madrassas, establish the credibility of
their degrees and check the quality of educations.

References

[1] Khalid, Saleem M. Deeni Madaris main Taleem. Institute of Policy Studies.
Islamabad.2005.p118

[2] Khalid, Saleem M. Deeni Madaris main Taleem. Institute of Policy Studies.
Islamabad.2005.p125

[3] Note for Record: A meeting was held in the office of Mr. Khalid Rehman,
Executive Director, Institute of Policy Studies, F-7 Markaz, Islamabad, with
the undersigned, on August 16, 2007.

[4] Pakistan: Religious Education Institutions: An Overview; IPS Task Force Report, 2002, Institute of Policy Studies, Islamabad p.22.

[5] Institute of Policy Studies Report. p32.

[6] National Education Census Pakistan. Ministry of Education and Statistics Division. Government of Pakistan. Islamabad.2006. p217

[7] National Educating Policy: 1998-2010: Government of Pakistan , Ministry of Education, Islamabad,1998 p 15

[8] National Educating Policy: 1998-2010: Government of Pakistan , Ministry of Education, Islamabad,1998 p 14

[9] Madrassa Reform Project PCI Part B, Page 4, 2003, Ministry of Education, Islamabad.

[10] Pakistan Religious Education Institutions, an Overview, IPS, Task Force Report: 2002, Institute of Policy Studies, Islamabad, Page 25, Table 1.2.

[11] National Education Census, Pakistan 2006, Ministry of Education and Statistics Division, Islamabad, Page 215.

[12] Haq, M. Ijazul, Bringing Madrassas into the Mainstream. The News International, July 15, 2007, Islamabad.

[13] National Education Census, Pakistan 2006, Ministry of Education and Statistics Division, Islamabad, Page 217.

7

WHY POLICY
IMPLEMENTATION FAILS?
Can it be replaced with success?

Most of the policies are difficult to measure. Some of the policies are deliberately avoided to be measured because of possibility or fear of negative results or extremely limited achievement in view of the resources and time invested in the policy implementation. It is not uncommon to note that the policy objectives are lofty, hence unachievable. Then there are issues of quantitative output. There are several aspects of policies that are extremely difficult to measure. One such example could be the social justice. The quality of life is another complex preposition for measuring in quantitative terms. However concerted efforts have to be made to identify the key performance indicators but this could only measure the policy processes and implementation[1]. Then there has to be separate sets of output and outcome indicators. If both these sets are available it becomes reasonably possible to measure policy performance. But it may not provide sufficient quantitative data but it needs to be measured and sometimes interfaced with quantitative indicators.

There are several factors for lack of proper implementation of policies which are often termed as reasons of policy failure. The situation varies from country to country but there are common threads which run across and lead to poor implementation hence policy failure.

Cause Analysis

Political Interference

The bureaucratic decision regarding the appointments, postings, transfer, and promotions emanate from political base. Employees are hired, irrespective of the suitability, qualification and experience for the position to appease different groups of politicians. Most of the contracts are awarded to political party workers ignoring the merit, or to relatives of high officials. The retired bureaucrats are hired as consultants on lucrative salaries and perks for achieving political mileage rather than seriously implementing the policy provisions. It is somewhat difficult to completely get away from political influences but it can be minimized to a level where the policy implementation processes do not suffer. It so happened in Pakistan that the appointments of chief executives of different public sector outfits were made in gross violation of merit. They were not even educated at college level. The chairman of Oil and Gas Regulatory Authority (OGRA) was appointed, who is the brother in law of very influential political worker, ignoring the criteria of educational qualifications, experience, honesty and morality. The result was that the chairman in span of few months misappropriated billions of Rupees and absconded. He has been nabbed from overseas. The amount of corruption by the Chairperson of OGDC is in billions as Rs:54.85 billions has been recovered from him.[2] Similarly another convict was appointed to a top slot bureaucratic position without having minimum qualification and experience. He was only a high school graduate.

Centralized Bureaucratic System

In the Federal system of government (like India, Pakistan, USA, etc.) there has always been an uneven relationship between the federation and federating units. The common debate and key reason of the conflict is that federal government feels that strong central government provides strength to the federating units. Whereas the Units (States, Provinces, Districts in Thailand) feel that central government can only be strong if the units are autonomous and powerful. There is no easy answer to this riddle. However each organ of the state needs to work in a synergy where the constitutional, political and economic interests are not overstepped by either side. The other issue is that of implementation gap. The preparation of national policy of any sector remains the prerogative of federal government but the implementation, in 90% of the cases, has to be done at the state level. The federal government is usually willing to shift the responsibility of implementation but very reluctant to delegate the commensurate authority and resources to the units. Hence the policy implementation becomes a victim of diarchy and the ownership of programs and project remain in dispute.

The policy preparation at federal level set objectives and guidelines without proper understanding of local situation and culture. Also the diversity of ground realities within each unit and intra units is enormous. Federal government feels that their role is to play as 'guardian angel' for the provinces where as the provincial governments and structure are convinced that they are autonomous entities and free to make policy decisions as it suits to each province.

Another important aspect or cause of conflict is the distribution of resources. There is mechanism which is available for resources distribution (in Pakistan) through National Finance Commission Award. The meeting of NFC Award needs to be held every year which must be participated by all the Chief Executives of states and Federal government is represented by minister of Finance on behalf of Chief executive of the country which is Prime Minister in case of Pakistan. But meetings are not held every year and even the decisions of NFC awards are not implemented.

Pressure of Time

There is an inherent problem in the preparation of policy in which the targets are inflated hence unrealistic whereas the time and resources are underestimated rather depressed. So at the outset, the implementation starts with poor planning. Secondly the ruling political party is always in a hurry to show tangible results in the form of deliverables during its tenure but certainly before the next election. The pressure tactics are employed on the implementation agencies where the required technical personnel are not available. The normal course is to select the personnel as per the rules and regulations. The qualification and experience required for implementation must be strictly adhered. As a practice neither the rules nor the prescribed qualifications are followed in the selection process. The non-compliance of rules, time pressure, over estimated and unrealistic targets and above all bad governance caps it all which has resulted into poor policy implementation.

Politics of Interest Groups

The role of interest groups politics cannot be limited to policy formulation. The groups i.e. labour unions or trade unions exert their influence to either stop or hinder the implementation of public policies. There could be various reasons for this role and behavior. One such example could be an environmental policy. This policy becomes an easy target because several policies and their implementation do not comply with the state regulations or evade industrial laws. This happens irrespective of developed and developing countries.

In the case of Pakistan another example could be that of the implementation of Education Policy. Despite reiteration and plans of compulsory primary education, it has never been implemented particularly in those pockets and villages of rural areas where the big landlords have land holdings and control the life and destinies of land labourers and tenants. They control their life in such a way that tenants are depended on landlords for their food security, decision about marriage of their children, economic earning and above all on their thought process. They cannot vote to anyone against the choice or decision of landlord of the area. In such a situation the educational institutions are not established in those areas. Hence the policy implementation has been hampered and enrollment remained depressed particularly for girls in primary education. Similarly literacy does not improve despite policy stipulations and allocation of funds. In brief it means that access to education has been deprived to poor or disadvantaged section of society specially in rural areas.

The influence exerted by Industrialist, especially on the formulation of import and export policies, tax regulations, exchange rates etc. usually effects poor people negatively. The role of other rich and powerful groups including the landlords is no different when it comes to fix the prices of food especially in the context of food items allowed by the government for import or export.

Role of Bureaucracy

Bureaucracy has been considered as a backbone of Public Policy implementation because of their Administrative and Management skills; professional training; well versed in procedural niceties and relevant experience. The bureaucracy is also aware of these strengths. However, it happens often that personnel working at the lower level of administrative structure tend to unionize for better pay structure, improved facilities and enhanced opportunities for promotion etc. The key reason for their demand is the inequalities and inequities between the higher bureaucracy and support staff. The higher bureaucracy is rewarded without resorting to any protest because the government knows well that it would be impossible to manage and administrator policies and day to day office work without their guidance and help. The struggle or demand of staff or lower bureaucracy may affect implementation negatively hence lead to policy failure. The attitude of higher bureaucracy is generally favorably in the policy implementation process. Their interests are well guarded by the political elite because the politicians (Ministers, Ministers of State, parliamentary secretaries, members of legislature) have to depend on bureaucracy. The politicians are generally not properly educated, lack experience of management, unaware of technical knowledge and above all do not have enough time and interest to get involved in the policy implementation process. It is important that legitimate and genuine interests of lower bureaucracy are well protected so that unionization could be minimized.

Poor Coordination

All the policies are formed and implemented with the coordination and cooperation of various ministries, divisions, departments and institutions. As an example health policy needs support from several other ministries which may include i.e. finance, planning & development, population welfare, environment, women and education. There are usually missing links in the administrative and bureaucratic setup which makes the policy implementation complex and difficult. There is always a fear of territory, as no ministry or department would allow to be over stepped by some other ministry. This means that coordination assumes an important role for which some mechanism have to be evolved and established on regular basis to avoid the problems of poor coordination. Sometime the misunderstanding could be due to the difference of perception between two ministries about the interpretations of certain policy stipulations which lead to conflict and results into policy failure. Some policies have major component which is funded by donors or lending agencies. Each organization providing finances follow its own financial rules and regulations hence the administrative ministry which is overall responsible for implementation of policy is caught up in very difficult and complex situation. The rules and guidelines of different ministries and funding agencies have to be followed that hampers the satisfactory progress of work.

Resource constraints

When the policy is announced the cost element is always directly relevant to achieve policy objectives. The policies for purpose of implementation make plans, develop programs and implement projects. In case of Pakistan the Five Year Development Plans are prepared which are further bifurcated into Annual Development Programs and then divided into different projects. These projects are the key instruments for policy deliverables. The costing of projects and program has been done professionally but very often the planned financial, technical and manpower resources have not been made available. At the time of annual budget announcement, a specific amount is allocated for the project but always followed by financial cuts because of different reasons. As a result the allocation becomes meaningless. The available financial resources released for the project implementation could be 30% less than what is planned and required.

Public Participation

The role of public participation is important in the implementation of most of the social sector policies. But the level of participation by the community remains negligible. The successful implementation of policies like health, education, literacy, environment etc. can benefit from the people living in those places or areas where the sub-components of policy in the shape of projects is implemented. Staff absenteeism is a chronic problem in rural areas for primary education and primary health care. The availability and presence of qualified teachers are critical for running a school and so is the doctor and paramedical staff for primary Health Care System. The people living in the vicinity of primary school and primary health care center can monitor the performance of these institutions and take corrective actions when required. They could keep a watchful eye on the staff and minimize frequent absenteeism. This could be done in collaboration with or guidance of the departmental staff. As a result the community would benefit from better quality of services. It is often observed that there has been a general lack of interest by the public in development activities being undertaken by the local government in their vicinities. However there has been a tendency of complaint and dissatisfaction by the community. The lack of will and interest to improve their surroundings in the context of development programs is quite apparent. It happens, both in rural and urban areas, that people are living very close to sewage broken pipes, garbage dumps and other filth but do not participate to mitigate the problem but only criticize the surroundings.

Capacity of a system

There has been a constant complaint about the non-availability of sufficient financial resources. This is going to remain so for most of the countries in view of the emerging problems of poverty, human insecurity, diseases and food deficiency. Pakistan is one of those countries with limited financial resources and poorly managed governance. This is manifest from the outcome of policy implementation which reflects that the financial resources made available for different projects and programs in various sectors have not been fully and properly utilized. The system of governance and management as well as the institutions and individuals responsible for the program and project planning and implementation do not have the capacity to use the available resources.

At the end of the financial year considerable amount allocated to health, education, population welfare, environment sectors remained unutilized and few weeks before the close of financial year it has to be diverted to other programs and projects. The situation in other sectors may be slightly better in terms of capacity and administrative responsibility but it still remains quite limited and need considerable improvement.

References

[1] For a comprehensive reading about KPIs & Evaluation: Khawaja, Sarfraz: Good Governance and Result Based Monitoring: Mr. Books: 200

[2] Daily 'Nawa-e-Waqat' Lahore: Sep 11, 2013: p1&8

BIBLIOGRAPHY

1. Aaron Wildavsky, Speaking Truth to power? New York: John Wiley, 1979

2. Allama Iqbal Open University, Islamabad: Commonwealth of Learning Executive MBA/MPA: Sc1 Public Policy, Code 5572: 2004

3. Anderson J.E: Public Policy Making: An introduction: Boston: Honghton Mifflin: 1990

4. Anderson, James E. Public Policymaking, 4th ed. Boston: Houghton Mifflin, 2000.

5. Aucoin, P. 1986. Organizational change in the Canadian machinery of government: From rational management to brokerage politics. Canadian Journal of Political Science 19(1):3-27.

6. Bardach, Eugene. A Practical Guide for Policy Analysis. New York: Chatham House, 2000.

7. Barrett, S. and D. Fudge, eds. Policy and action: Essays on the implementation of pubic policy. London: Methuen. 1981.

8. Bartlett, Donald L., and James B. Steele. America: Who Stole the Dream. Kansas City: Andrews and McMeel. 1996.

9. Bickers, Kenneth N., and John T. Williams. Public Policy Analysis: A Political Economy Approach. Boston: Houghton Mifflin, 2001.

10. Boston, J., J. Martin, J. Pallot, and P. Walsh. Public Management: The New Zealand model. Auckland: Oxford University Press. 1996.

11. Bridgeman, P. and G. Davis. Australian policy handbook. 2d ed. Sydney: Allen & Unwin. 1998.

12. Considine, M. Public Policy: A critical approach. Melbourne: Macmillan. 1999.

13. Conway, M. Margaret. Women and Public Policy. Washington, DC: CQ Press, 1994.

14. Corbett, D. Australian public sector management. 2d ed. Sydney: Allen & Unwin. 1996.

15. Dearlove, J. and P. Saunders. Introduction to British politics: Analysing a capitalist democracy. 2d ed. Cambridge: Polity Press. 1991.

16. Derthick, Martha. New Towns in Town, Washington, Urban Institute, 1972

17. Dr. Ashfaque H. Khan: "Poverty number revised": The News International, Islamabad: May 8, 2012

18. Dr. Muhammad Yaqub: "What to expect in the next Budget 2011-2012": The News International, Islamabad: May 8, 2012

19. Dunn, William N. Public Policy Analysis, 2nd Ed. Englewood Cliffs, NJ: Prentice Hall, 1994.

20. Dye, Thomas R.: Understanding Public Policy, Prentice Hall, New Jersey: Upper saddle River: 2002

21. Earl Latham "The Group Basis of Politics", in Political Behaviour ed. Heinz Eulan San, Elders veld aid Morris Janowitz, New York, Free Press, 1956

22. Edwards, M. Social policy, public policy: From problem to practice. Sydney: Allen & Unwin. 2001

23. Graig, Laurene. Health of Nations: An International Perspective on US Health Care. Washington, DC: CQ Press, 1999.

24. Han, C. and M. Hill: The Policy process in the modern capitalist state. Brighton: Wheatsheof: 1984

25. Heidenleimer, A.J. Heclo, H, Adams, C.T: Comparative public policy. The politics of social choice in America, Europe and Japan: New York: St Martin's press, Inc. 1990

26. Hogwood, B.W and L.A. Gunn: Policy Analysis for the real World: Oxford: Oxford University Press: 1984

27. KAUTILIYA: Kautiliya Arthasatra: translated in English by R.P. Kangle; then translated in Urdu from English by Shan-ul-Haq Haqee: Karachi: Taxes Printers: 1991

28. Khawaja, Sarfraz: Good Governance and Result Based Monitoring: Poorab Academy, Islamabad: 2011

29. McMaster, J.C. Implementation Analysis: An overview: In new developments in public sector management: Concept papers and reports. Canberra: Australian National University. 1979.

30. National Commission on Excellence in Education. A Nation at Risk. Washington, DC: U.S. Government Printing Office, 1983.

31. Pressman, J. Waldavsky, A. Implementation: Berkeley: University of California: 1973

32. S.S. Nagel: The Policy Studies Handbook, Toronto: D.C. Heath & co. 1980

33. Sapru, R.K: Public Policy: Art and Craft of Policy Analysis: New Dehli: PHI Learning: 2010

34. Siddiqi, M: Governance in Islam: New Dehli: Maxford Books: 2006

35. Stewart, R.G. Public policy: Strategy and accountability. Melbourne: Macmillan. 1999.

36. The State of the World's Children 2011: UNICEF: United Nations Children Fund: New York: 2011.

37. Thomas R. Dye: Understanding Public Policy, upper Saddle River, New Jersey: 2002

38. Turner, M and D. Hulme: Governance, administration and development: Making the state work: London Macmillam: 1997

39. Vedung, Evert. Public Policy and Program Evaluation. New Brunswick, NJ: Transaction Books, 1997.

40. Wayne Hayes, Ph.D: 5/26/2009:
http://Profwork.org/pp/study/define.html

41. Wholey, Joseph S. Evaluation and Effective Public Management. Boston: Little, Brown, 1982.

42. Wildavsky, A. Speaking truth to power: The art and craft of policy analysis. New Brunswick: Transaction. 1987.

INDEX

Sarfraz Khawaja

About the Author

Sarfraz Khawaja completed his Master's Degree with distinction from University of the Punjab, Lahore and started teaching in a college. He competed in the Central Superior Services (CSS) Examination and was offered the position to join custom service but opted for academics. Sarfraz Khawaja earned his PhD degree from University of Missouri, Columbia, USA and then joined University of Wisconsin, USA as a faculty member. He also taught at Government College Lahore, (Now University). His other teaching assignment was that of Chief Instructor (Professor) at the Civil Services Academy, Lahore. He served as Deputy Educational Advisor in the Ministry of Education, Government of Pakistan and Director, Academy of Educational Planning and Management, Islamabad. His work experience extends to UNICEF as Planning Monitoring and Evaluation Officer. He also worked for UNFPA as Management Advisor. His latest assignment was Monitoring and Evaluation specialist in Planning Commission, Government of Pakistan.

He has been consultant to several International Agencies some of which include Swiss Development Cooperation (SDC), Asian Development Bank (ADB), Plan International, The World Bank, UNICEF, USAID, Aga Khan Educational Foundation. He was principal Research Partner in the BRIDGES Project carried out in collaboration with Harvard University, USA (1988-1990). He has been a visiting speaker at Allama Iqbal Open University, Quaid-i-Azam University, NIPA, Foreign Services Academy, and National Defence College, Islamabad (Now University).

Public Policy: *Formulation Implementation Analysis*

It resonates that Pakistan is not short of public policies. That may be the situation if the policy is seen as hybrid declaration of reactive statements by the chief executive or head of the state. Public policy is a sacred trust, a commitment of the stake holders and an instrument of public support for the well being of its people and advancement of the country. If these two things do not combine than the policy existence is farce and misleading.

In most of the developing countries like Pakistan public policy has been used as a vehicle of growth and hardly entailed change. Most of the policies related to different ministries and departments in Pakistan have this problem, because of the legacy of colonial rule in which social institutions and state policy were used as an instrument of repression to perpetuate power. Every situation was perceived as a law and order problem which could disrupt the revenue collection by the state apparatus.

The excitement of independence and sovereignty was so over whelming that structure and design of social institutions and public policy were not modified. The changed status of the society, not only in geographical sense, but more so in the context of social, political and economic development, the needed institutions to meet the demands of a new country were neither created nor developed.

The needs and expectations of the new polity were not compatible with the existing state institutions. The resulting chaos and mismanagement is the manifestation of conflict between the development process which presupposes to work for societal needs and the state policy which is dominated to protect the interest of elite groups. The state institutions whether dealing with the governance of the native subjects or the dispensation of justice, the operations of finances or the functions of civic amenities worked primarily through force, coercion, nepotism or any other such means.

Some other publications of the author

- **Good Governance and Result Based Monitoring**
  Poorab Academy, Islamabad.   ISBN: 978-969-8121-07-5: 2011
- **Governance and poverty in Pakistan: some reflections 2000-2006.**
  Mr. Books, Islamabad.   ISBN: 978-969-8121-06-8: 2007
- **Education Evaluation and Monitoring: Concepts and Techniques**
  Mr. Books, Islamabad.   ISBN: 978-969-8121-06-8: 2001
- **Non-Formal Education: Myth or Panacea for Pakistan**
  (Won the National Book Foundation Award)
  Mr. Books, Islamabad.   ISBN: 978-969-8121-04-8: 1990
- **Planning of Basic Education in Pakistan – 1989**
  Academy of Educational Planning and Management, Islamabad
                          ISBN: 969-444-064--5: 1989
- **Innovative Programmes of Basic Education - 1989**
  Policies and Plans Review 1947-89 – (Case Study of Pakistan):
  UNICEF, Islamabad.
  Basic Education for All: policies and plans review. 1947-89.
  UNICEF, Islamabad.
- **Promotion of Girls Education in the Context of Universalization of Primary Education, 1985.** UNESCO, Bangkok.
- **Primary Education in Pakistan and other Asian Countries: 1986.**
  Ministry of Education, Islamabad
- **Foreign Funding of Primary Education – (A Case Study of Pakistan). 1989.** UNICEF, Islamabad.
- **Technical Education: Its Relevance to Job Market: 1987.**
  Academy of Educational Planning and Management, Islamabad.
- **Sikhs of the Punjab.**
  A study of Confrontation and Political Mobilization 1900-1925:
  1985. Modern Book Depot, Islamabad.
- **Nasser: A Soldier among Diplomats, 1976.**
  Progressive Publishers, Lahore.

Email: sarfrazshk@yahoo.com

DEDICATION
COMMEMORATION

I am writing this note to commemorate the sad demise of my mentor (Guru), Professor N.G. Barrier, who left for his heavenly abode about two years ago. I worked under his able guidance and supervision for four years while pursing my graduate studies to earn doctoral degree in the Department of History at the University of Missouri, Columbia, Missouri USA. First time I called Prof. Barrier from the Columbia airport on January 2, 1976 when I reached from Pakistan to be his student at the University. It was frosty cold evening. In a brief chat he told me to get a taxi from the airport, which would cost me two US$ (actually there was a van which was taking several students to the campus) to take me to the down town and precisely at Tiger Motel on Broadway. It was brief journey, hardly any traffic on the road and here I was in front of the Motel trembling with piercing cold to which I was not aware off. I checked in the motel and went to my room trying to sleep which was nowhere near to me. I was mostly thinking about the person with whom I have to work for several years and I have tuition fee of only one semester and absolutely no money to go back anywhere.

Next morning I went to the University and had a first meeting with this venerable man who was completely different than what I thought. A man with haggard beard, golden spectacles, very sharp eyes, wearing almost yesterday's clothes, his office was burdened with books, reports and all other print material for reading and research loaded with information is such a way that it seems almost impossible to find a book, paper or reference which may be needed. But that was not what it seemed. Prof. Barrier in a flash of moment would find the book, report, record or any other information which he wanted me to read. He smoked pipe (smoking was quite popular and pipe smoking was favorite, ask Prof. Wallace) which seems quite worn out and he pushes the tobacco in the pipe with his fingers, took few puffs and restlessly moved to another errand. He offered me coffee in a cup which to our traditions was not clean because it had many coffee spots and look quite old. But his talk was so engaging and inspiring that my coffee mug lost its significance of causality. He briefed me about the courses I was about to take this semester and few hints about the life in the city. I reluctantly told him that I was a lecturer in prestigious college of my country which he already knew both the institution and my position. This gave me confidence and sense of creditability of a person with whom I have to work so closely for the next four years. These were small things for him but he did all that in great way that made him great. He was indeed a great man and scholar of exceptional ability. I don't consider appropriate to comment on his scholastic endeavors and achievements, some of which he tried to transfer to me and I think to every other student who was keen to become part of that height.

During the course of my first semester I told Prof. Barrier about my financial position so he immediately provided the opportunity to work for few hours per week at his book store (South Asia Books) mostly packing/unpacking, putting stamps on packets and any other related work. This work enabled me to pull on with the weekly grocery which I required. My performance in four graduate courses was very good during the first semester hence he recommended me for Department Assistantship which I was awarded before the close of the first semester. But his judgment was redeemed with my final result of first semester. I was awarded A's in all four courses.

This espoused confidence in me though I was still living below the poverty line but it was a jubilant time. Then came the summer and I opted to go to the summer school for which I have no tuition fee to pay. I decided to apply for the Curators Fellowship and requested Prof. Barrier to write a reference for me which he willing agreed. Limited number of fellowship and quite big number of foreign students was the challenge. The reference letter by my adviser was very helpful in which he wrote to the Foreign Student Coordinator of UMC that 'Sarfraz doggedly competed in the first semester and proved his competence as high level graduate student I am confident that given the opportunity he would add to our existing knowledge of history'. I got the fellowship initially for the summer of 1976 but it continued every summer till I wrote that it was no longer needed because I have completed all my course work, qualified in my comprehensive examination and doing research and also writing dissertation. I was little apprehensive while working at the dissertation for two reasons. Firstly my typing was terrible hence I had to write the draft chapters with a pen and pass on to him and secondly I was not sure whether my style of writing would fit with his standards. It turned out to be a surprise when I turned in the first hand written chapter to him and after a week. I met him in his office. He was in good mood and we have a nice meeting and above all he was happy with the work I have done. I continued my efforts and completed the work in about eight months and rest is history.

During the period I was working on the dissertation I started applying for teaching job in some universities around USA. I got an interview call from the University of Wisconsin and told Prof Barrier. I was more surprised than him about this development and he astonished me by saying that the University of Wisconsin has by now asked him for my reference to which he has already responded. I don't know what he wrote about me but I went for interview and selected the same day for the faculty position. I came back to Columbia as my wife and son was there and also to pack for the shifting. My wife, Aqila student of Prof. Wallace, graduated from the Department of Political Science and was nursing our one year old son Ahsan. Next day she went to her Department of Political Science to meet some of her professors and shared the news of my job at Wisconsin. One of her professors asked Aqila as how your husband got this job, and she said God help him. The Professor said to her "Please tell your God to help us". By telling these things is to commemorate the departure of my mentor and everyone has to go at a time which the almighty has fixed. Prof Barrier you are in heavens and have played your innings in the best possible way by making the lives easier of fellow human beings.

Sarfraz Khawaja
Ph.D (University of Missouri, USA)